Box Additi

Adding using the box method will expand your student's knowledge in math. Students will leran how to apply the expanded form method then add using the traditional method to achieve the answers. This workbook has 76 days of practice sheets to help students excel.

(Answer key inlcuding in the back of the workbook)

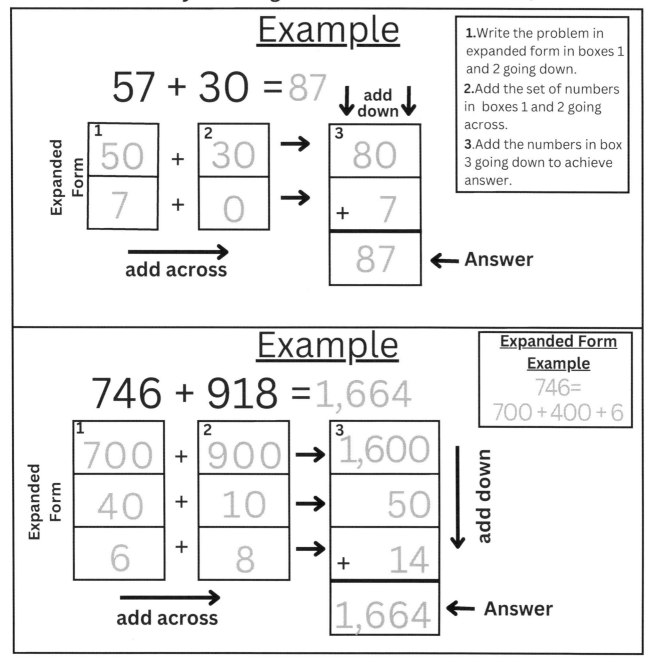

Box Expanded Form Double Digit Adding

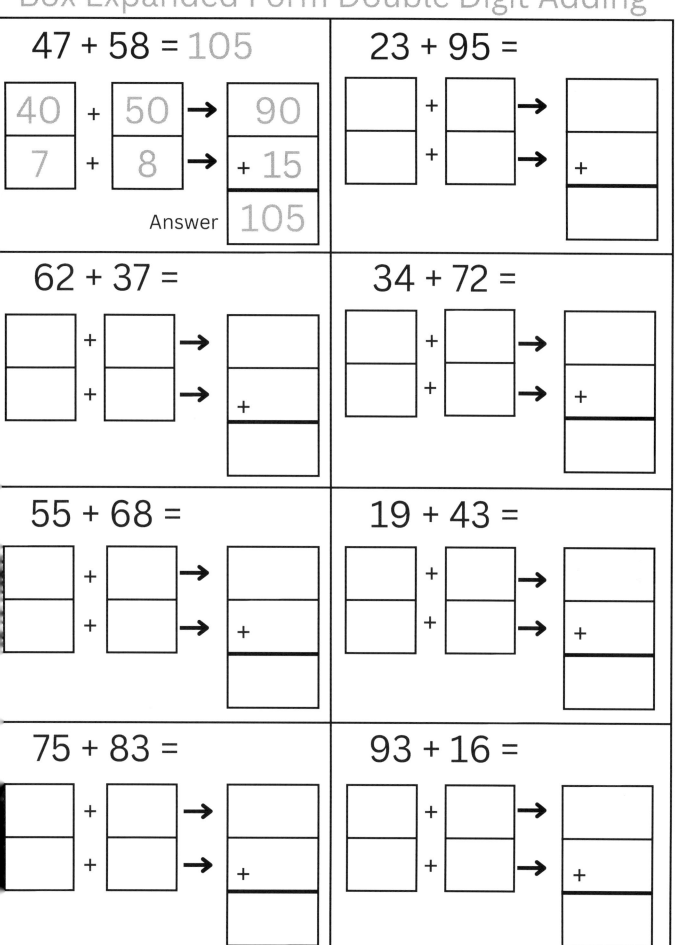

47 + 58 = 105

| 40 | + | 50 | → | 90 |
| 7 | + | 8 | → | + 15 |

Answer 105

23 + 95 =

62 + 37 =

34 + 72 =

55 + 68 =

19 + 43 =

75 + 83 =

93 + 16 =

Day 1

Box Expanded Form Double Digit Adding

36 + 74 = 110

30	+	70	→	100
6	+	4	→	+ 10

Answer: 110

43 + 86 =

	+		→	
	+		→	+

72 + 25 =

	+		→	
	+		→	+

95 + 13 =

	+		→	
	+		→	+

61 + 37 =

	+		→	
	+		→	+

58 + 62 =

	+		→	
	+		→	+

82 + 40 =

	+		→	
	+		→	+

27 + 56 =

	+		→	
	+		→	+

Box Expanded Form Double Digit Adding

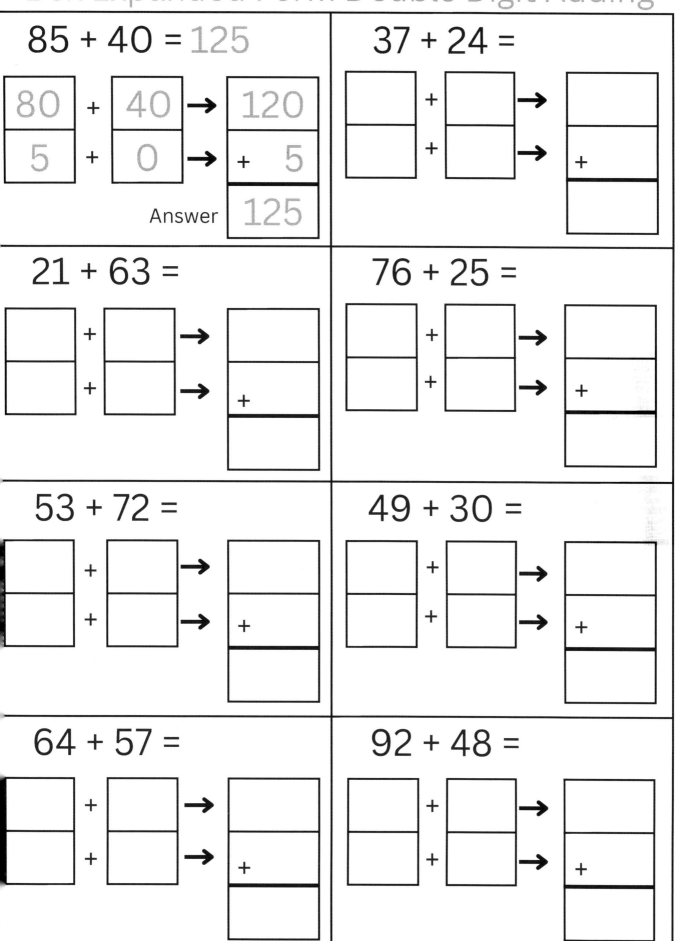

85 + 40 = 125

| 80 | + | 40 | → | 120 |
| 5 | + | 0 | → | + 5 |

Answer 125

37 + 24 =

21 + 63 =

76 + 25 =

53 + 72 =

49 + 30 =

64 + 57 =

92 + 48 =

Box Expanded Form Double Digit Adding

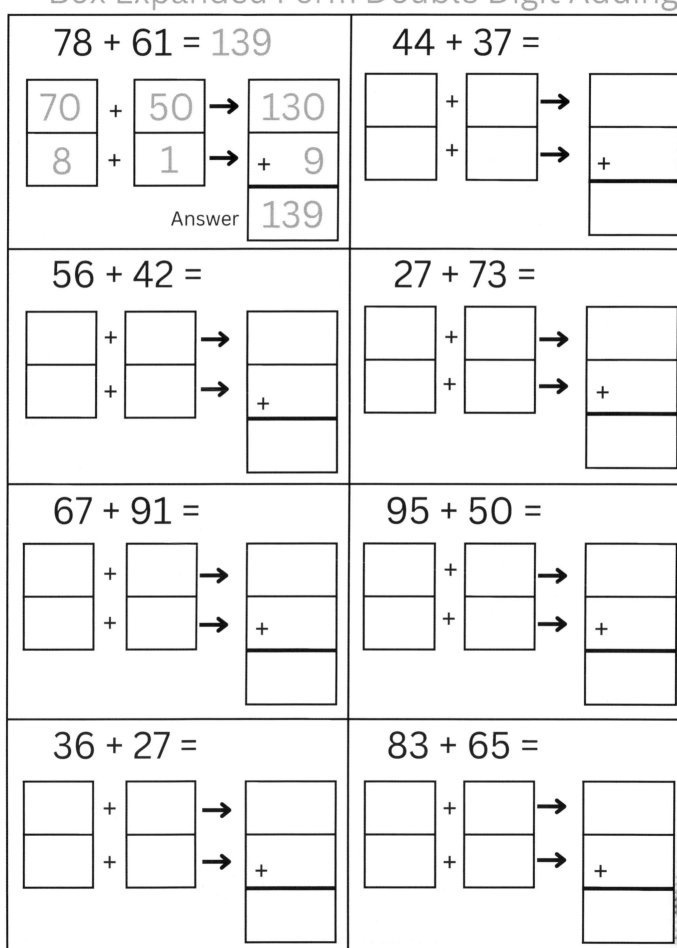

78 + 61 = 139

| 70 | + | 50 | → | 130 |
| 8 | + | 1 | → | + 9 |

Answer: **139**

44 + 37 =

56 + 42 =

27 + 73 =

67 + 91 =

95 + 50 =

36 + 27 =

83 + 65 =

Box Expanded Form Double Digit Adding

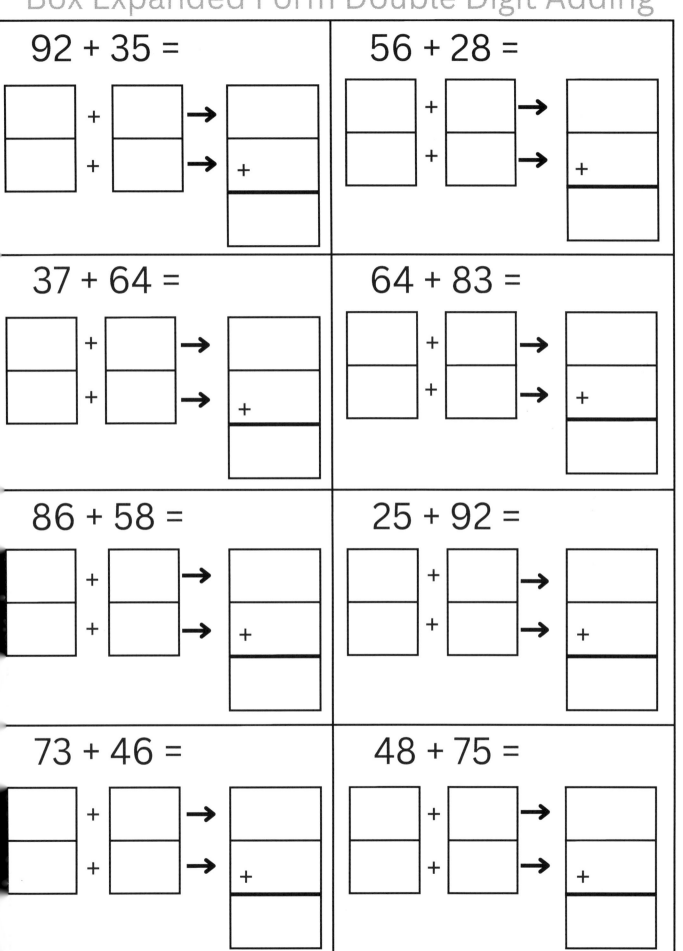

92 + 35 =

56 + 28 =

37 + 64 =

64 + 83 =

86 + 58 =

25 + 92 =

73 + 46 =

48 + 75 =

Box Expanded Form Double Digit Adding

59 + 43 =

84 + 35 =

27 + 61 =

46 + 83 =

77 + 24 =

93 + 57 =

33 + 87 =

65 + 98 =

Box Expanded Form Double Digit Adding

32 + 94 =

74 + 63 =
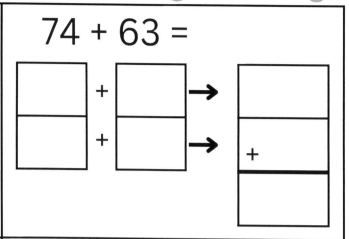

56 + 37 =
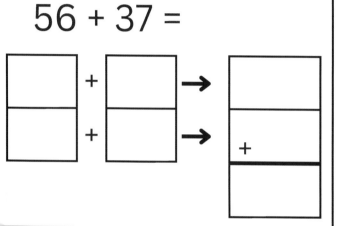

89 + 56 =
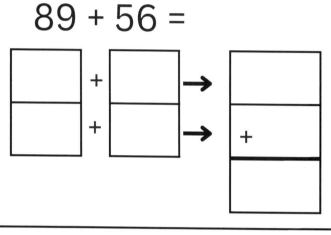

67 + 85 =
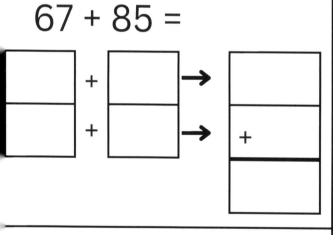

34 + 78 =
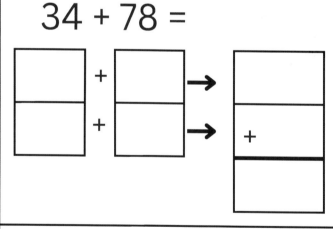

48 + 29 =
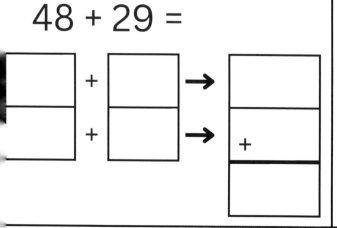

94 + 47 =
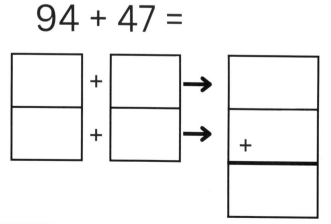

Box Expanded Form Double Digit Adding

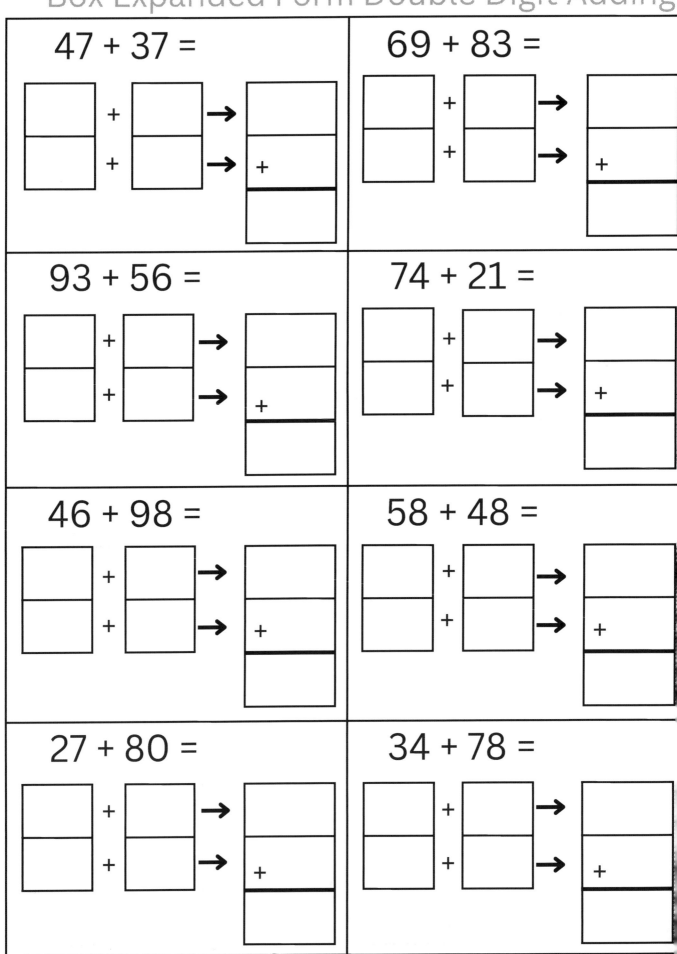

47 + 37 =

69 + 83 =

93 + 56 =

74 + 21 =

46 + 98 =

58 + 48 =

27 + 80 =

34 + 78 =

Box Expanded Form Double Digit Adding

62 + 88 =

38 + 47 =

54 + 95 =

21 + 31 =

87 + 59 =

73 + 77 =

40 + 60 =

99 + 99 =

Box Expanded Form Double Digit Adding

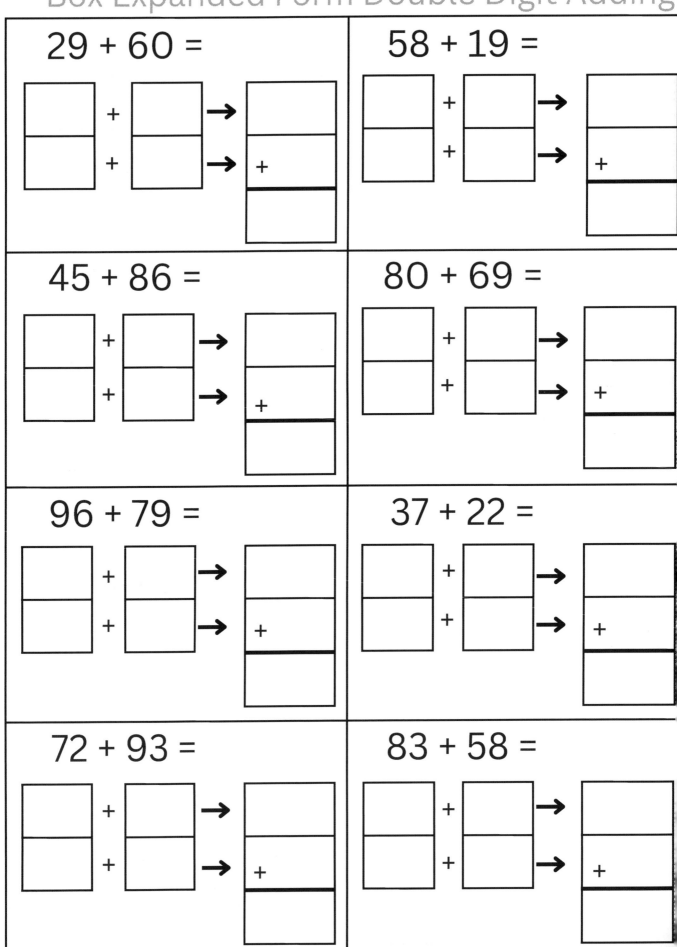

29 + 60 =

58 + 19 =

45 + 86 =

80 + 69 =

96 + 79 =

37 + 22 =

72 + 93 =

83 + 58 =

Box Expanded Form Double Digit Adding

57 + 41 =

32 + 98 =

76 + 66 =

95 + 80 =

44 + 69 =

68 + 54 =

89 + 37 =

24 + 71 =

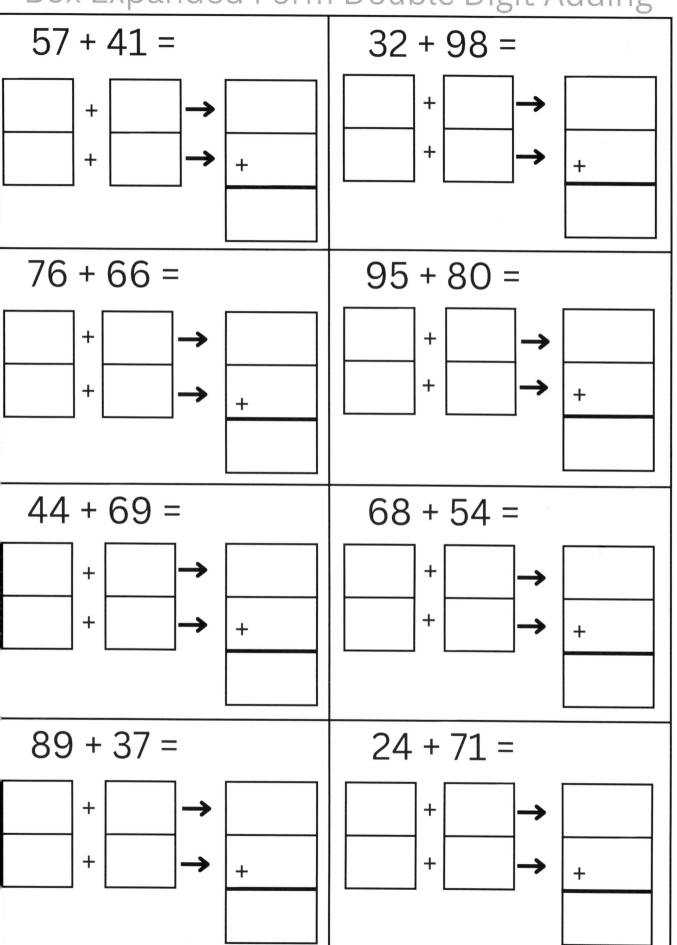

Box Expanded Form Double Digit Adding

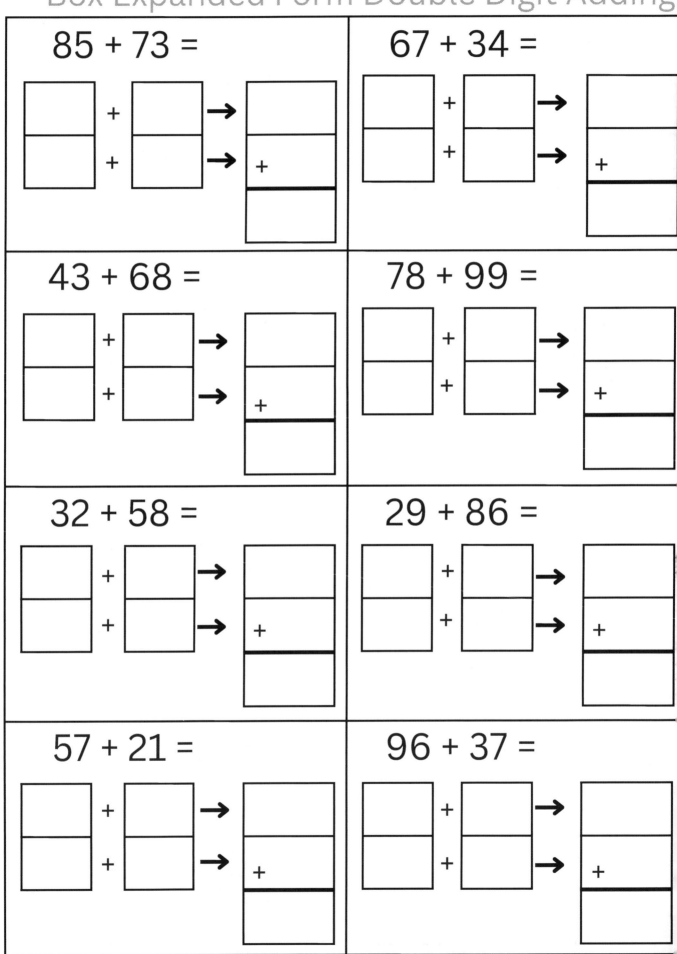

85 + 73 =

67 + 34 =

43 + 68 =

78 + 99 =

32 + 58 =

29 + 86 =

57 + 21 =

96 + 37 =

Box Expanded Form Double Digit Adding

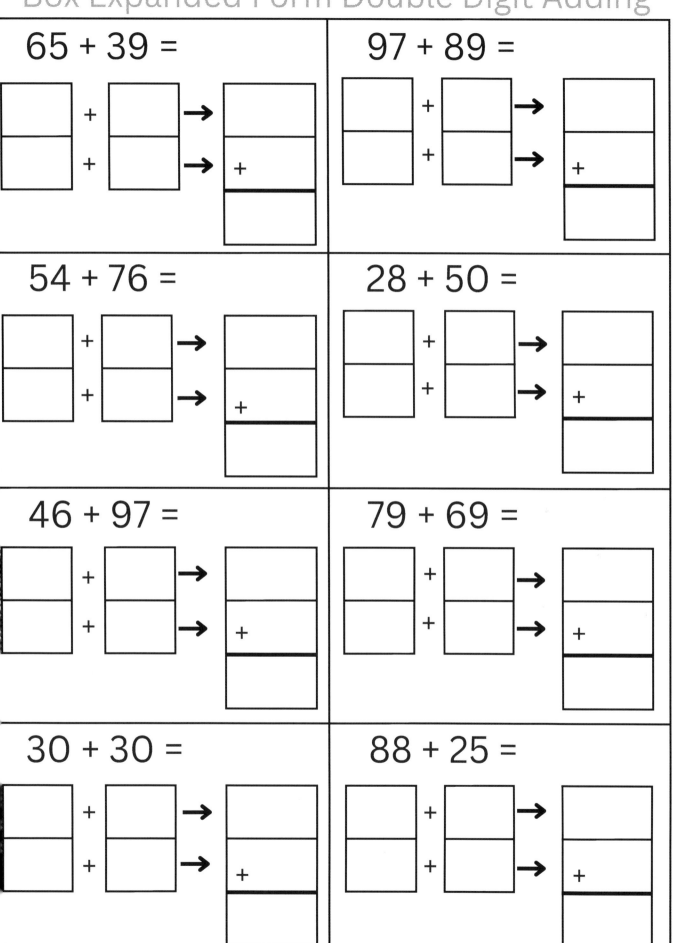

65 + 39 =

97 + 89 =

54 + 76 =

28 + 50 =

46 + 97 =

79 + 69 =

30 + 30 =

88 + 25 =

Box Expanded Form Double Digit Adding

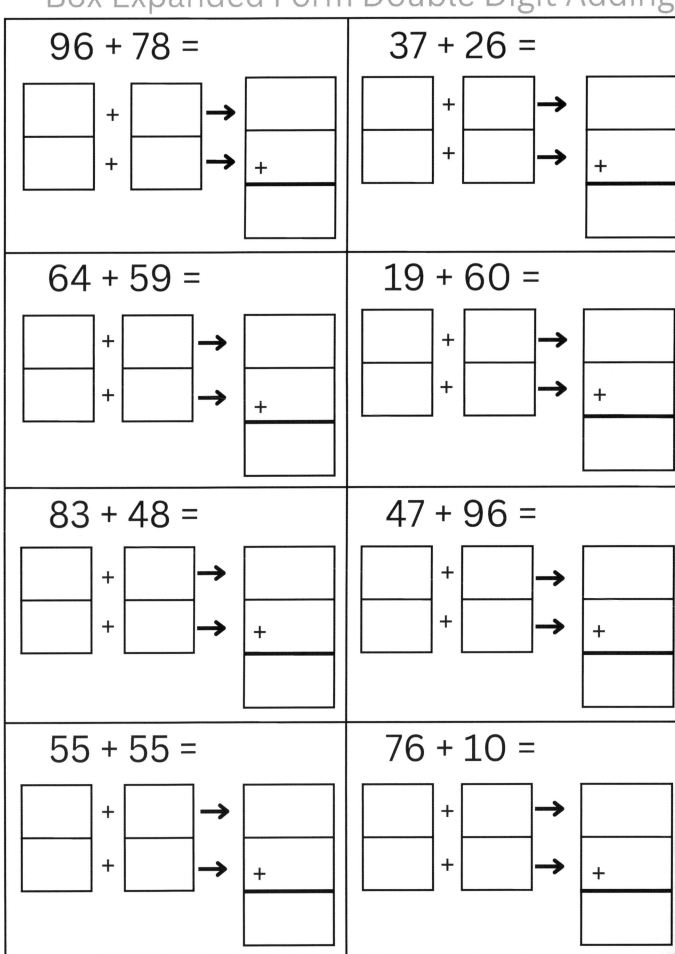

96 + 78 =

37 + 26 =

64 + 59 =

19 + 60 =

83 + 48 =

47 + 96 =

55 + 55 =

76 + 10 =

Box Expanded Form Double Digit Adding

15 + 19 =

28 + 27 =

96 + 97 =

53 + 58 =

37 + 34 =

74 + 78 =

85 + 86 =

69 + 63 =

Box Expanded Form Double Digit Adding

38 + 51 =

54 + 77 =

72 + 48 =

96 + 82 =

89 + 76 =

12 + 34 =

63 + 49 =

47 + 99 =

Box Expanded Form Double Digit Adding

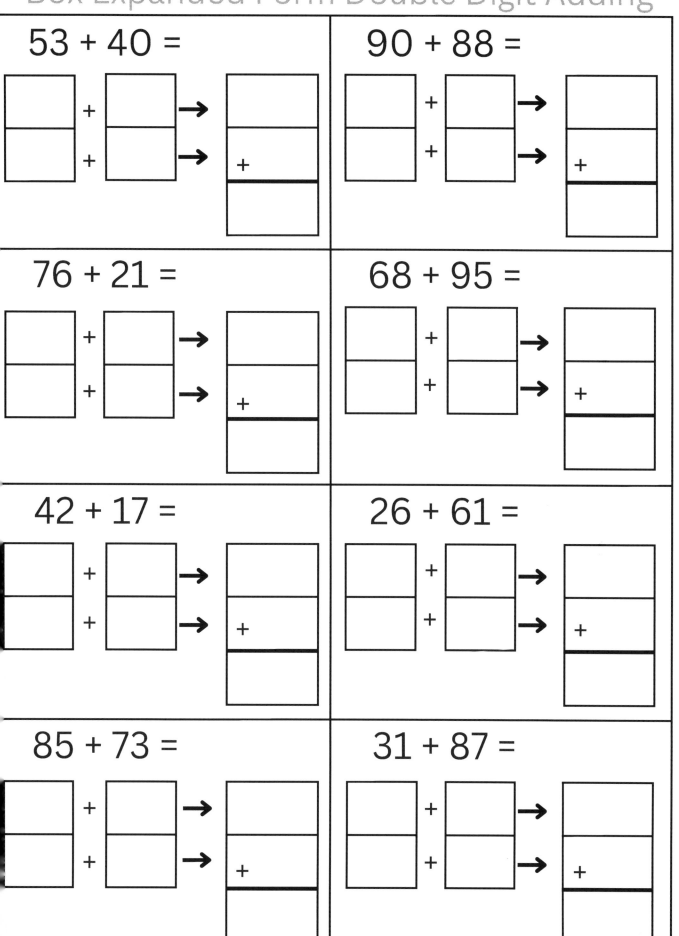

53 + 40 =

90 + 88 =

76 + 21 =

68 + 95 =

42 + 17 =

26 + 61 =

85 + 73 =

31 + 87 =

Box Expanded Form Double Digit Adding

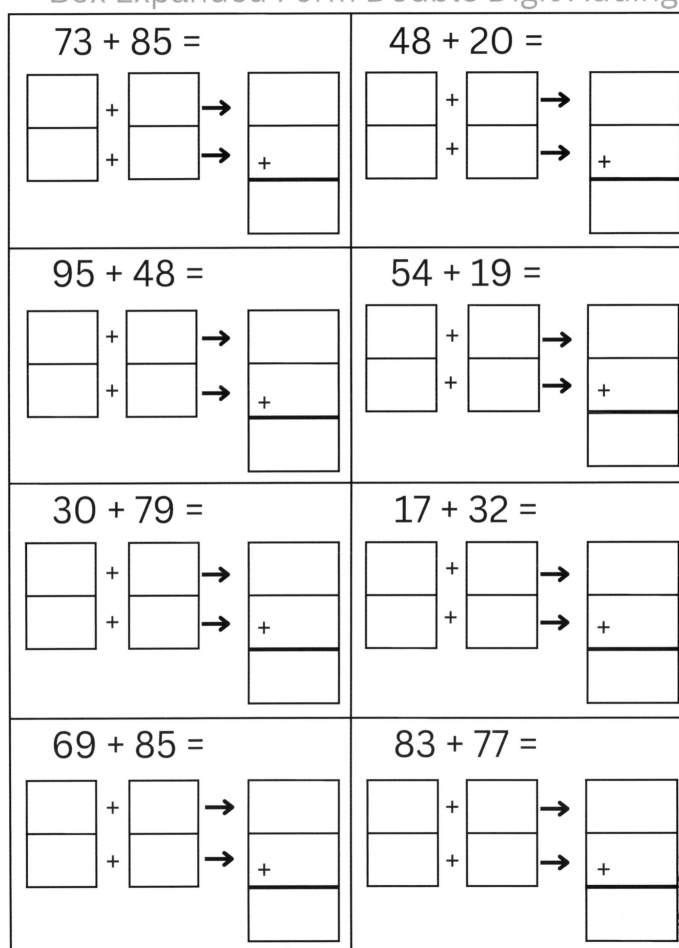

73 + 85 =

48 + 20 =

95 + 48 =

54 + 19 =

30 + 79 =

17 + 32 =

69 + 85 =

83 + 77 =

Box Expanded Form Double Digit Adding

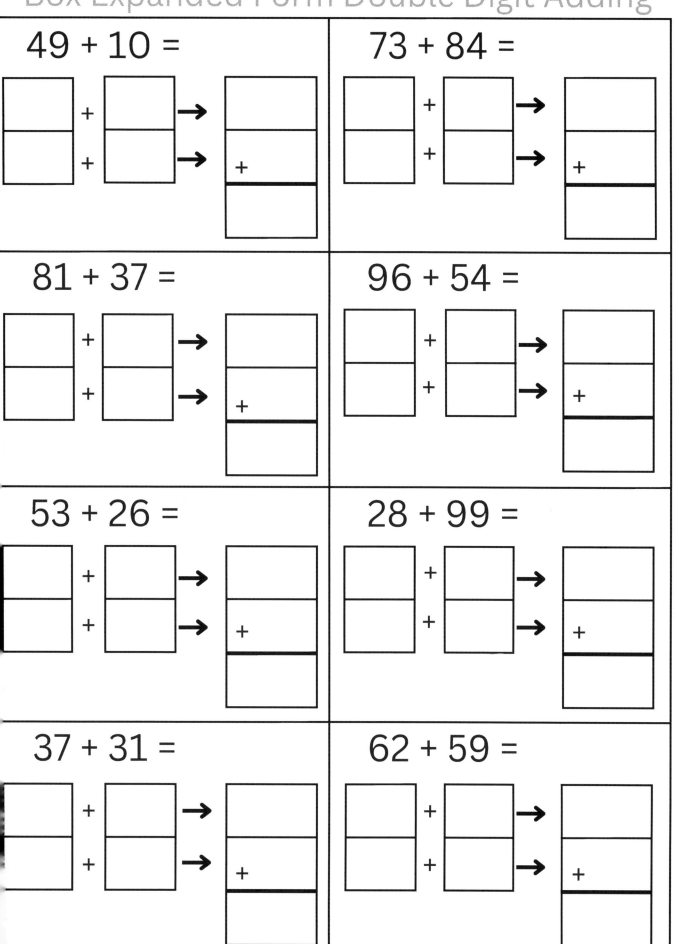

49 + 10 =

73 + 84 =

81 + 37 =

96 + 54 =

53 + 26 =

28 + 99 =

37 + 31 =

62 + 59 =

Box Expanded Form Double Digit Adding

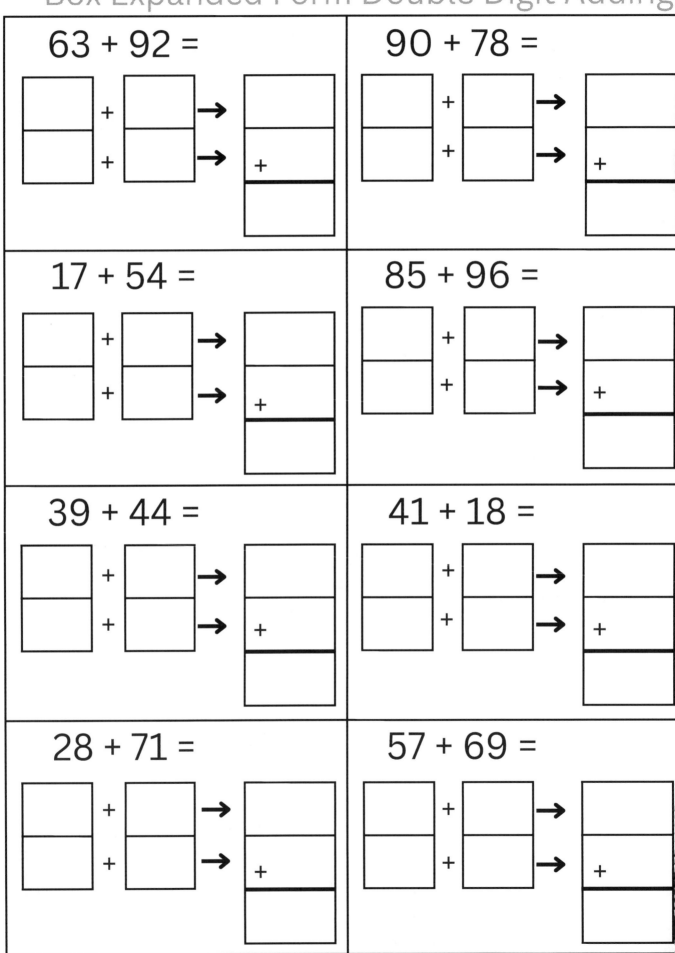

63 + 92 =

90 + 78 =

17 + 54 =

85 + 96 =

39 + 44 =

41 + 18 =

28 + 71 =

57 + 69 =

Box Expanded Form Double Digit Adding

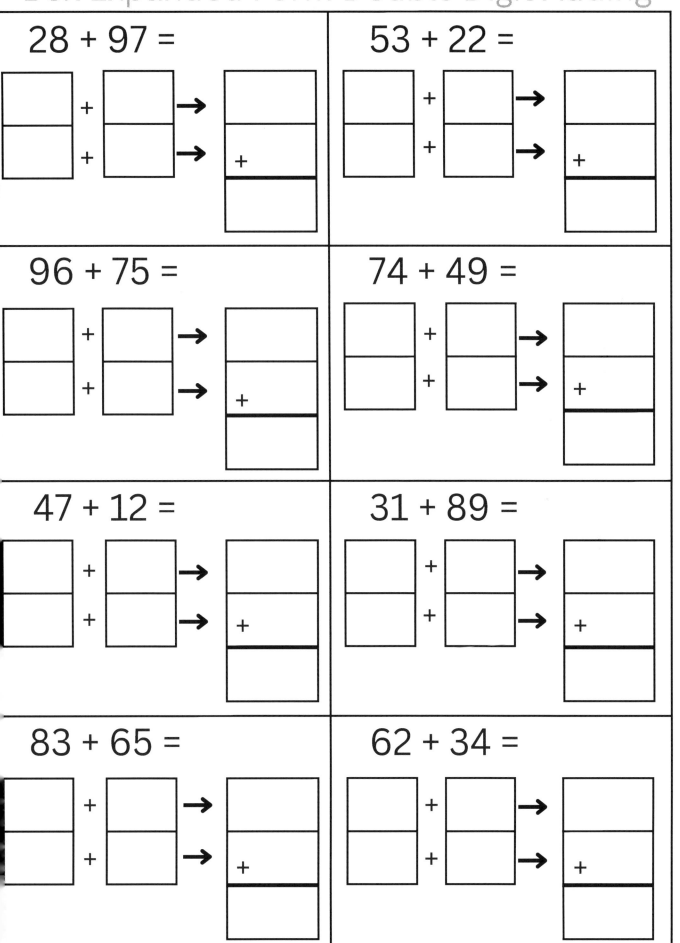

28 + 97 =

53 + 22 =

96 + 75 =

74 + 49 =

47 + 12 =

31 + 89 =

83 + 65 =

62 + 34 =

Box Expanded Form Double Digit Adding

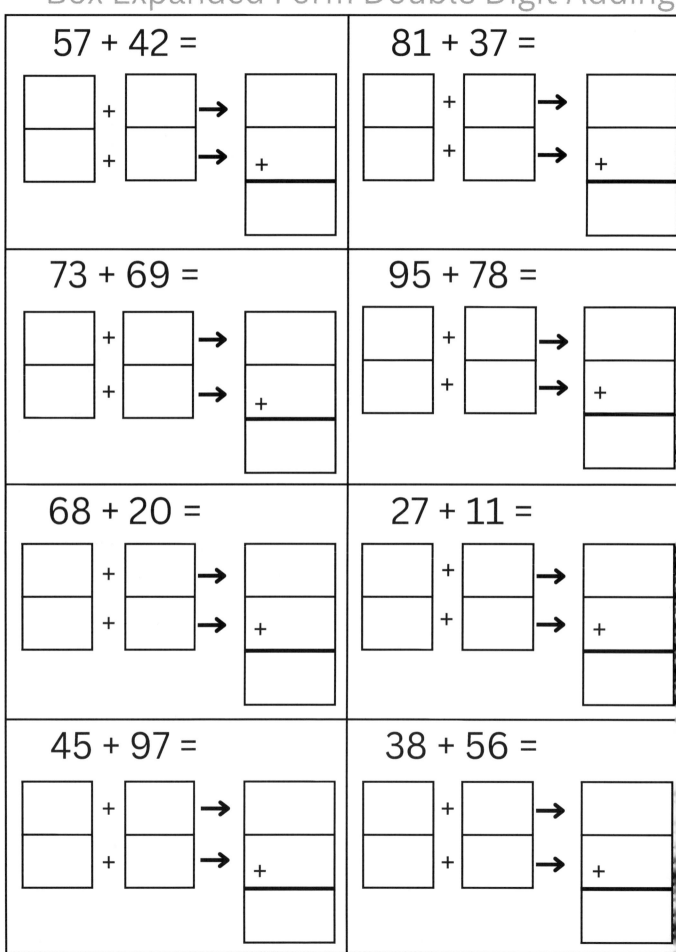

57 + 42 =

81 + 37 =

73 + 69 =

95 + 78 =

68 + 20 =

27 + 11 =

45 + 97 =

38 + 56 =

Box Expanded Form Double Digit Adding

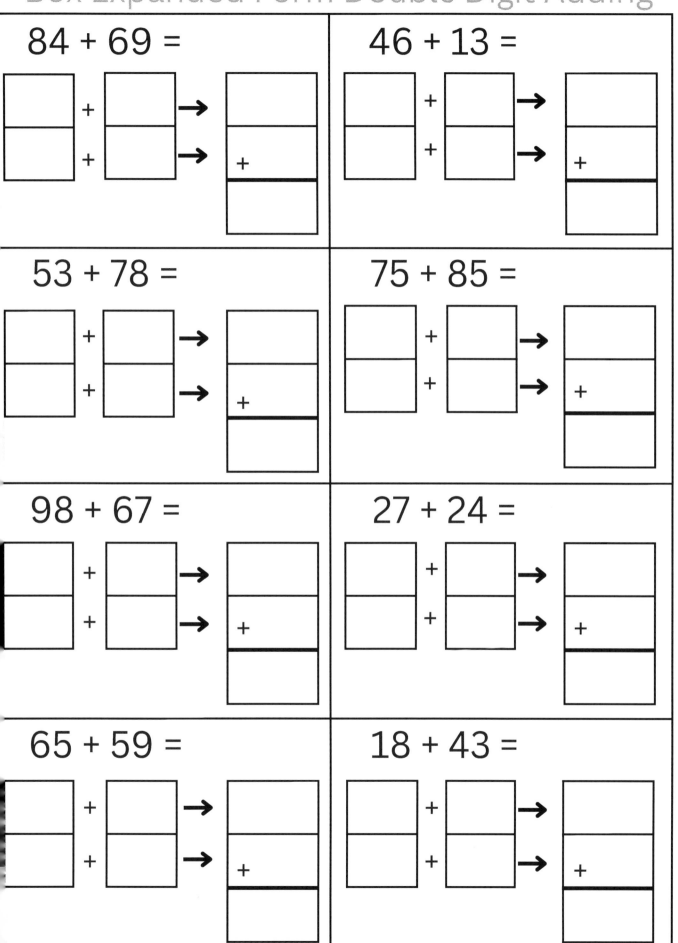

84 + 69 =

46 + 13 =

53 + 78 =

75 + 85 =

98 + 67 =

27 + 24 =

65 + 59 =

18 + 43 =

Box Expanded Form Double Digit Adding

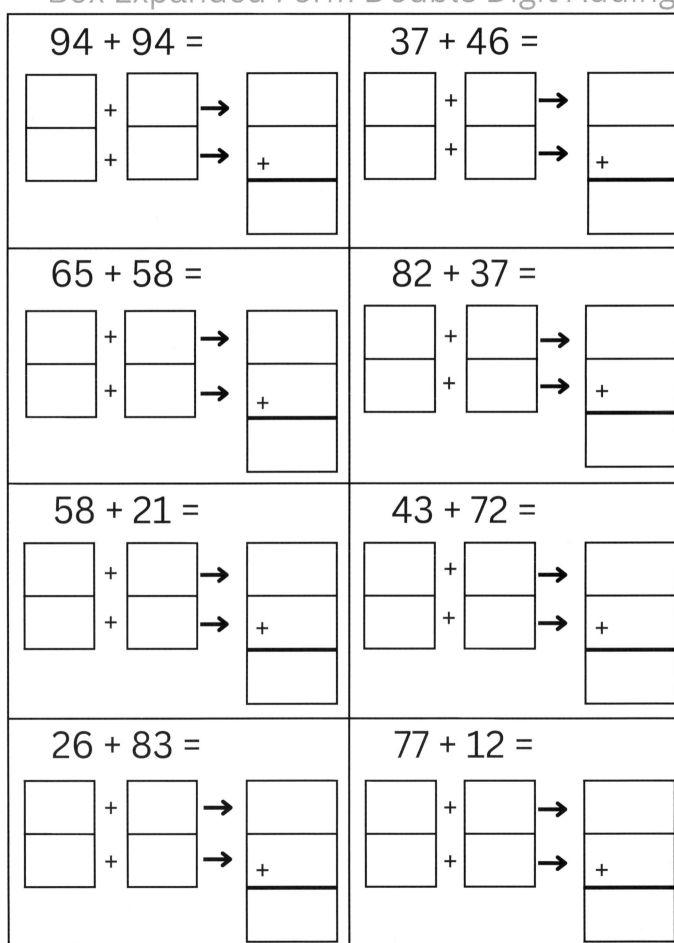

94 + 94 =

37 + 46 =

65 + 58 =

82 + 37 =

58 + 21 =

43 + 72 =

26 + 83 =

77 + 12 =

Box Expanded Form Double Digit Adding

78 + 64 =

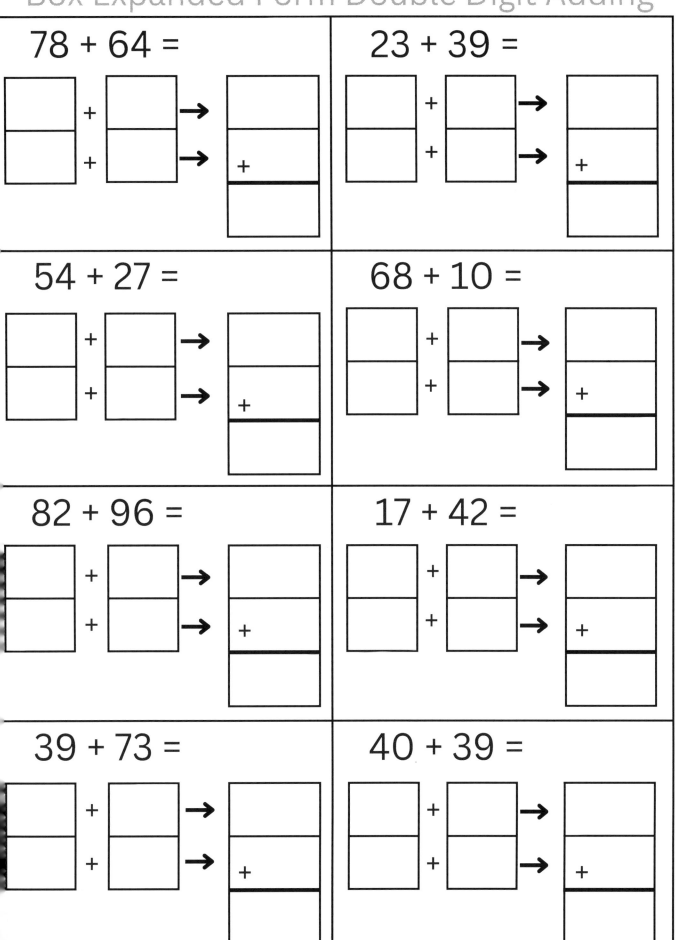

23 + 39 =

54 + 27 =

68 + 10 =

82 + 96 =

17 + 42 =

39 + 73 =

40 + 39 =

Box Expanded Form Double Digit Adding

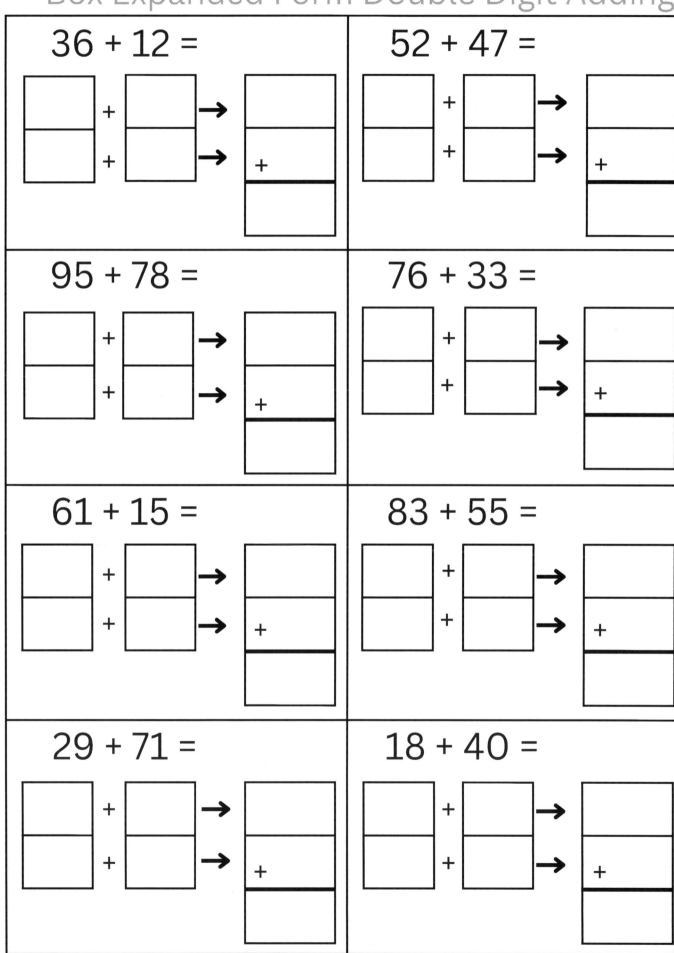

36 + 12 =

52 + 47 =

95 + 78 =

76 + 33 =

61 + 15 =

83 + 55 =

29 + 71 =

18 + 40 =

Box Expanded Form Double Digit Adding

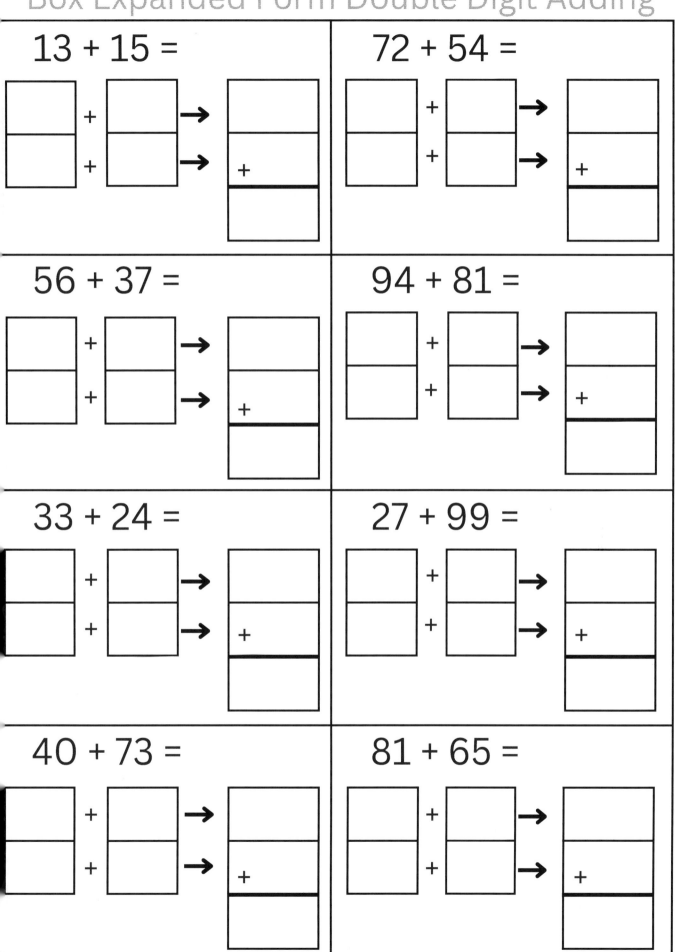

13 + 15 =

72 + 54 =

56 + 37 =

94 + 81 =

33 + 24 =

27 + 99 =

40 + 73 =

81 + 65 =

Box Expanded Form Double Digit Adding

47 + 23 =

63 + 94 =

15 + 34 =

82 + 97 =

76 + 65 =

48 + 10 =

31 + 54 =

50 + 83 =

Box Expanded Form Double Digit Adding

84 + 72 =

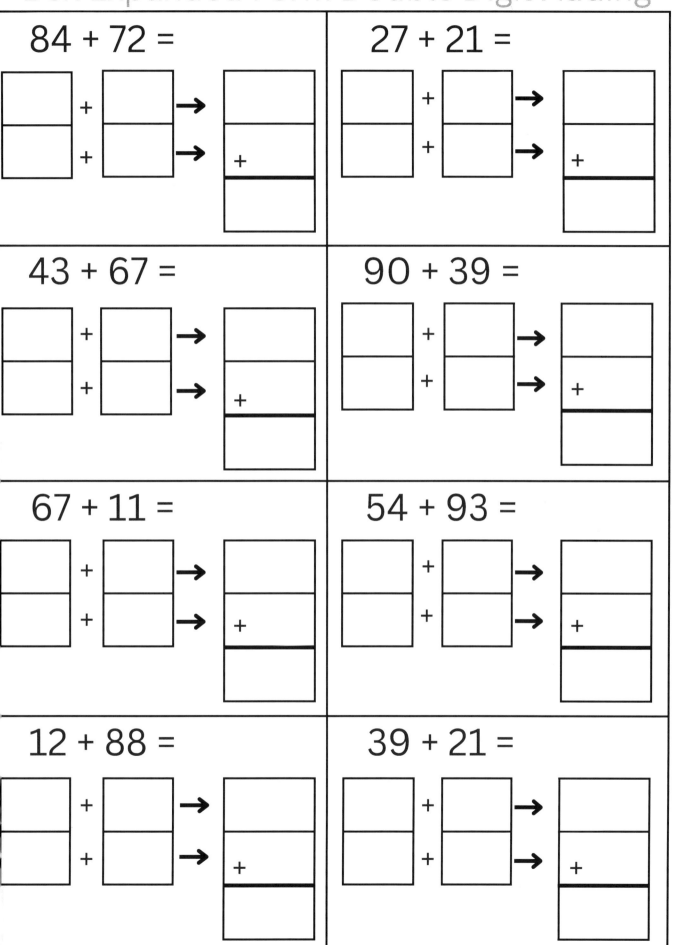

27 + 21 =

43 + 67 =

90 + 39 =

67 + 11 =

54 + 93 =

12 + 88 =

39 + 21 =

Box Expanded Form Double Digit Adding

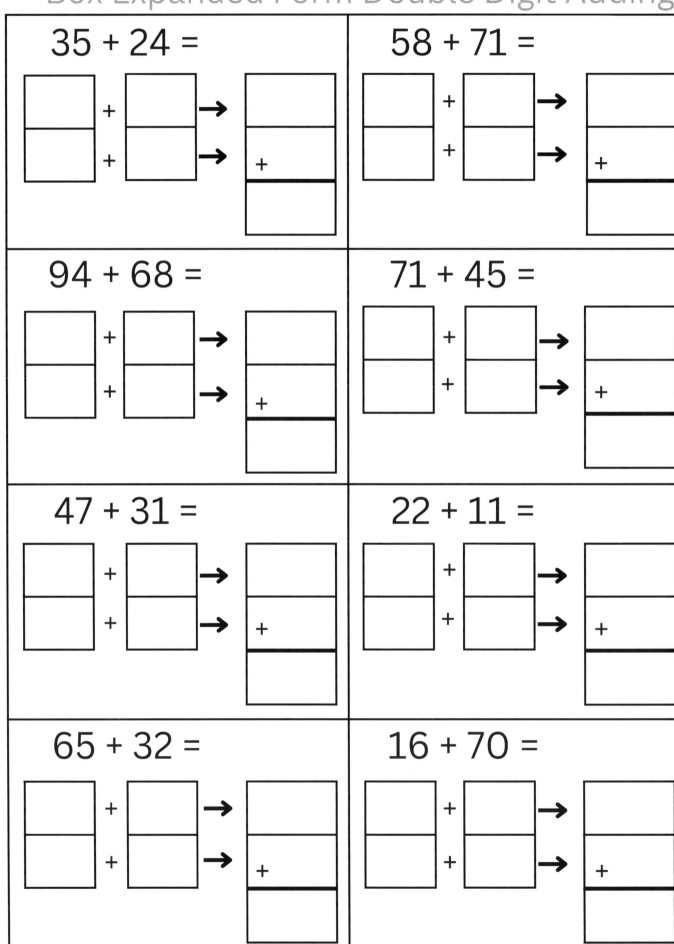

35 + 24 =

58 + 71 =

94 + 68 =

71 + 45 =

47 + 31 =

22 + 11 =

65 + 32 =

16 + 70 =

Box Expanded Form Double Digit Adding

55 + 23 =

74 + 20 =

89 + 75 =

35 + 21 =

68 + 26 =

43 + 19 =

94 + 32 =

70 + 30 =

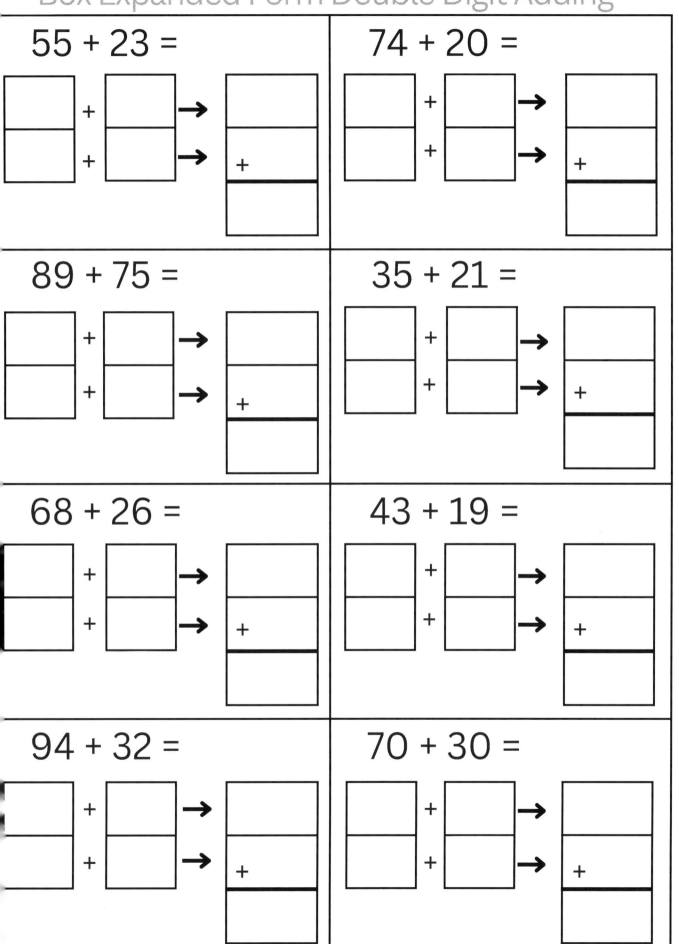

Box Expanded Form Double Digit Adding

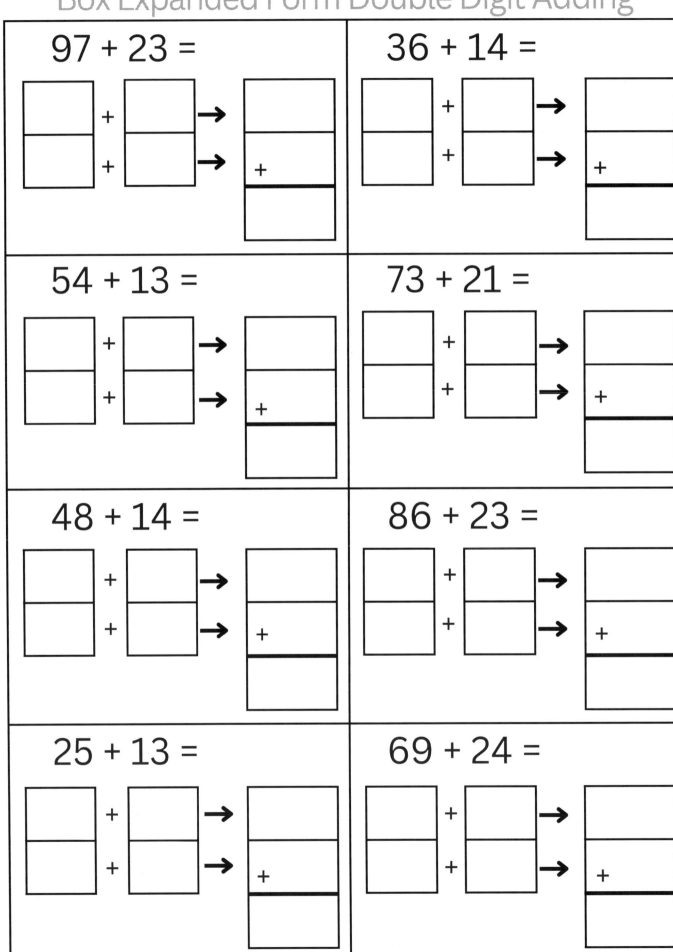

97 + 23 =

36 + 14 =

54 + 13 =

73 + 21 =

48 + 14 =

86 + 23 =

25 + 13 =

69 + 24 =

Box Expanded Form Double Digit Adding

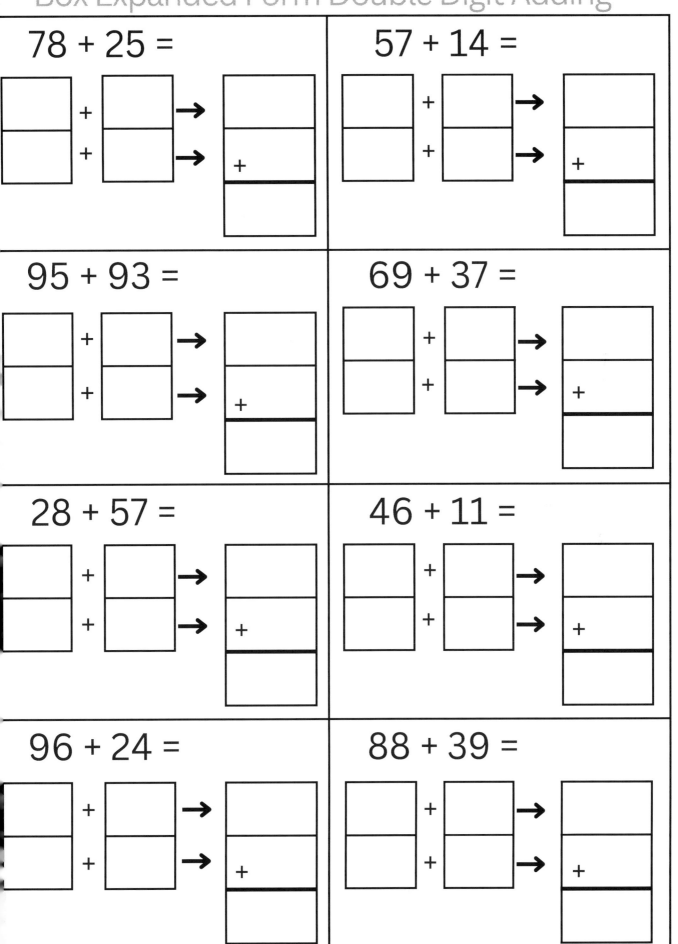

78 + 25 =

57 + 14 =

95 + 93 =

69 + 37 =

28 + 57 =

46 + 11 =

96 + 24 =

88 + 39 =

Box Expanded Form Double Digit Adding

36 + 62 =

57 + 75 =

84 + 93 =

23 + 10 =

14 + 62 =

92 + 74 =

67 + 48 =

79 + 28 =

Box Expanded Form Double Digit Adding

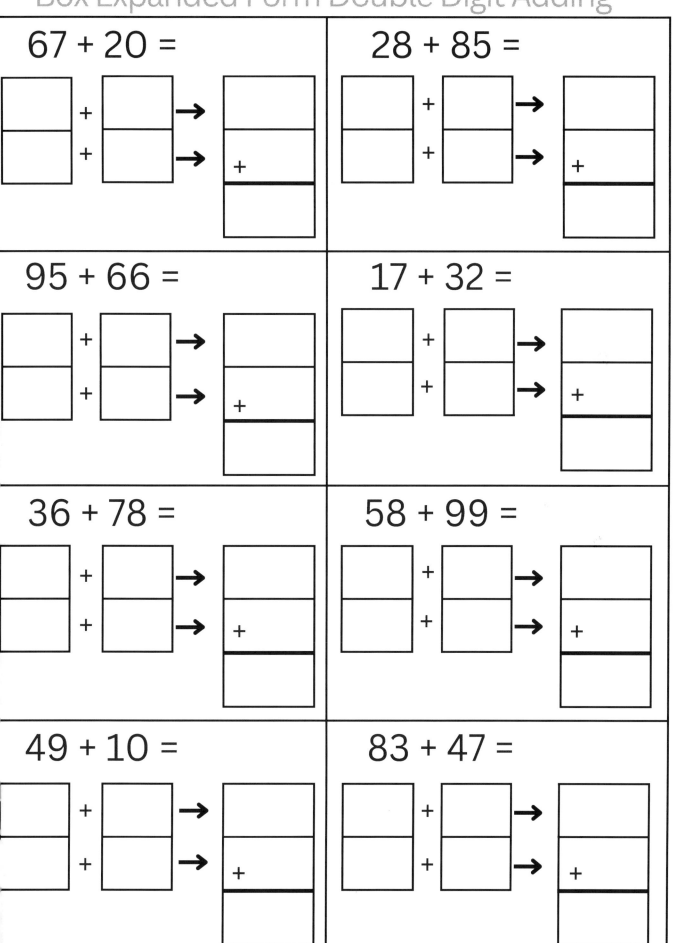

67 + 20 =

28 + 85 =

95 + 66 =

17 + 32 =

36 + 78 =

58 + 99 =

49 + 10 =

83 + 47 =

Box Expanded Form Double Digit Adding

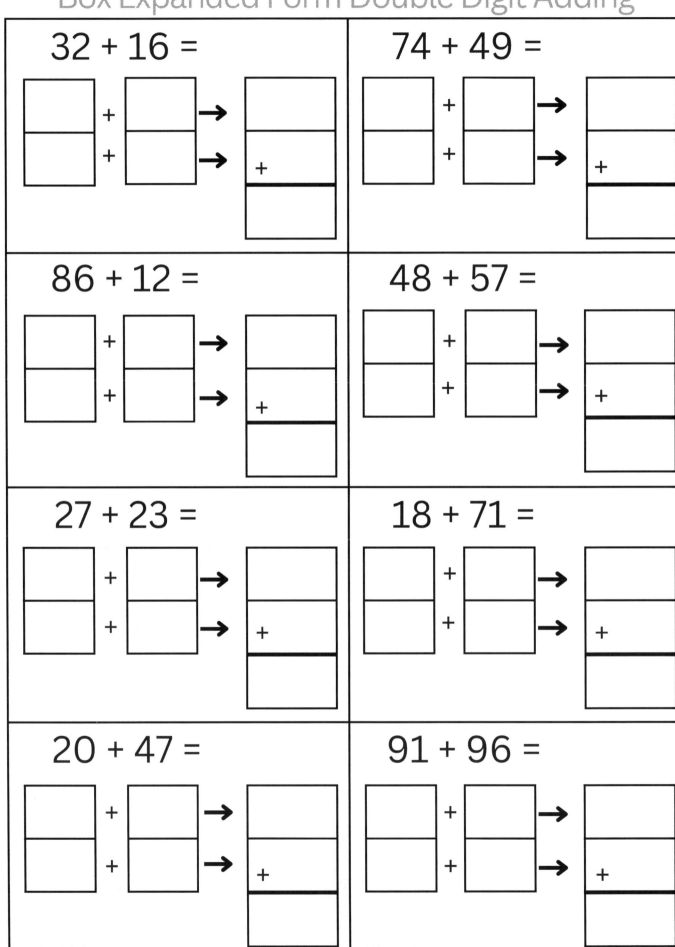

32 + 16 =

74 + 49 =

86 + 12 =

48 + 57 =

27 + 23 =

18 + 71 =

20 + 47 =

91 + 96 =

Box Expanded Form Double Digit Adding

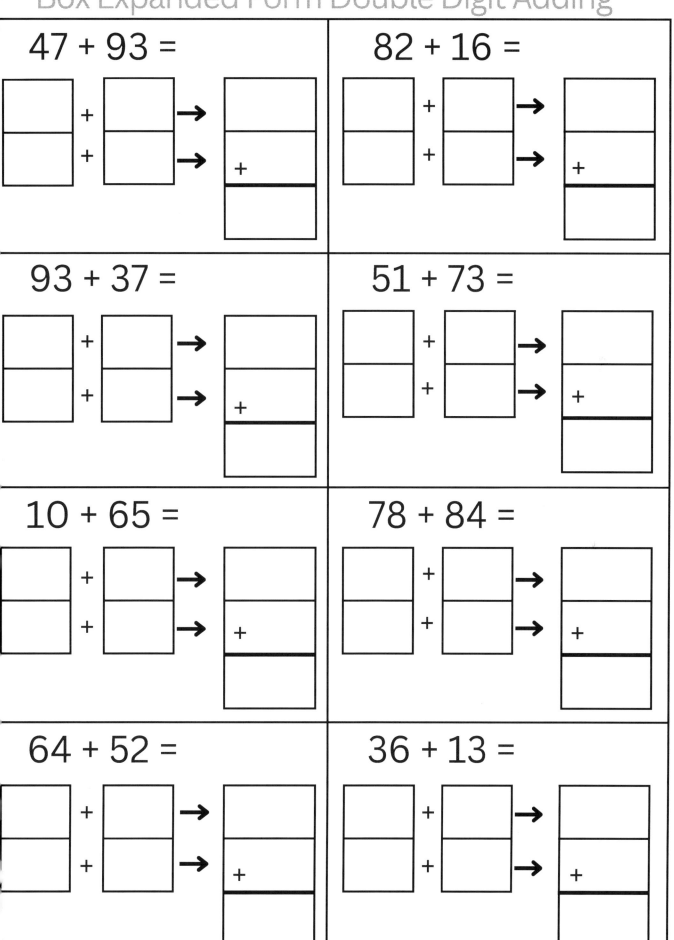

47 + 93 =

82 + 16 =

93 + 37 =

51 + 73 =

10 + 65 =

78 + 84 =

64 + 52 =

36 + 13 =

Box Expanded Form Triple Digit Adding

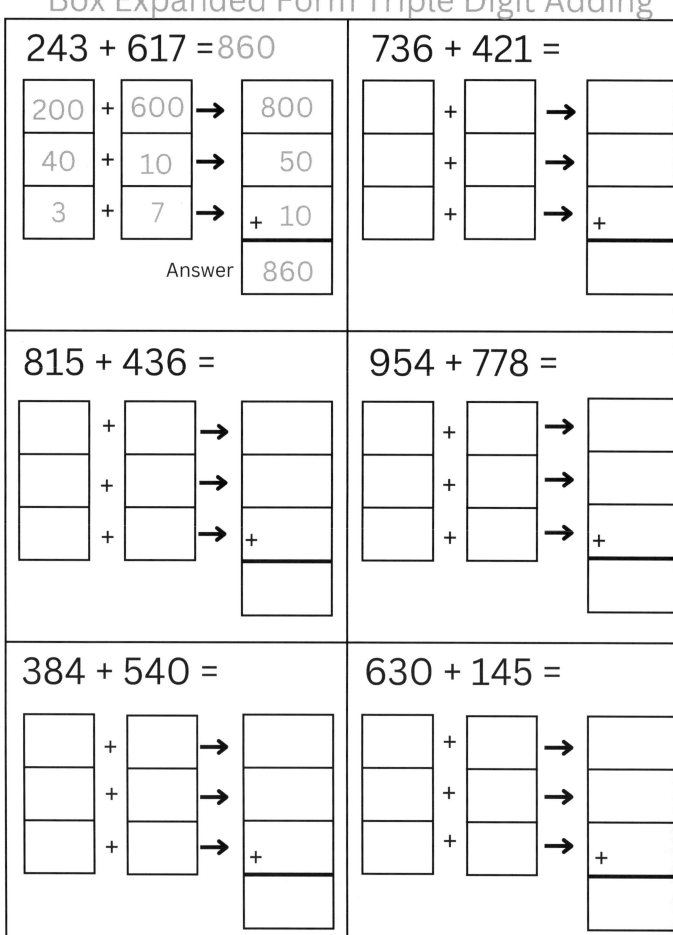

243 + 617 = 860

200	+	600	→	800
40	+	10	→	50
3	+	7	→	+ 10

Answer 860

736 + 421 =

815 + 436 =

954 + 778 =

384 + 540 =

630 + 145 =

Box Expanded Form Triple Digit Adding

408 + 725 = 1,133

400	+	700	→	1,100
0	+	20	→	20
8	+	5	→	+ 13

Answer 1,133

295 + 631 =

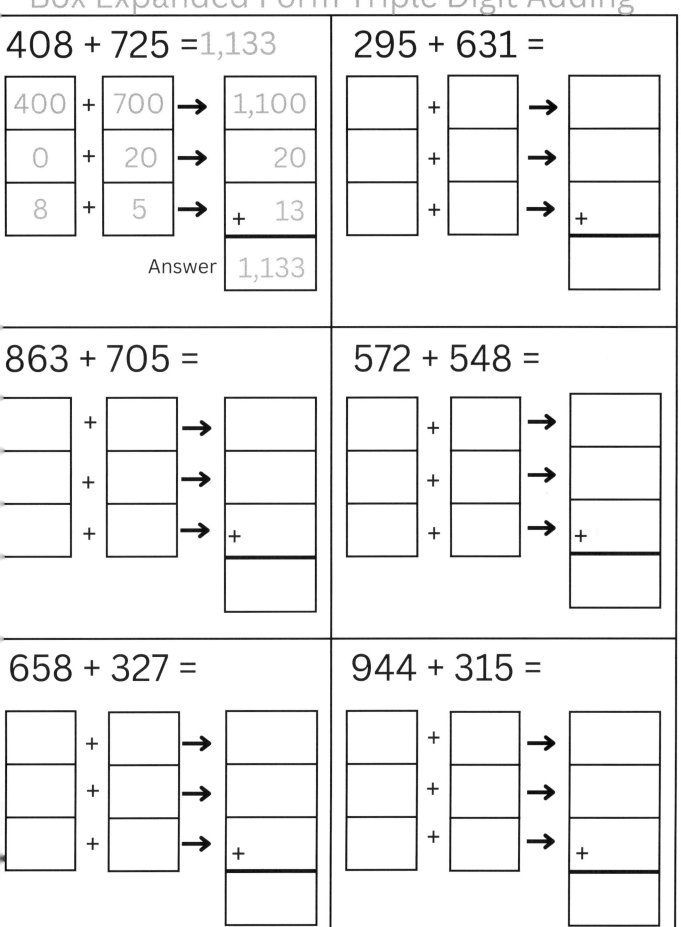

863 + 705 =

572 + 548 =

658 + 327 =

944 + 315 =

Box Expanded Form Triple Digit Adding

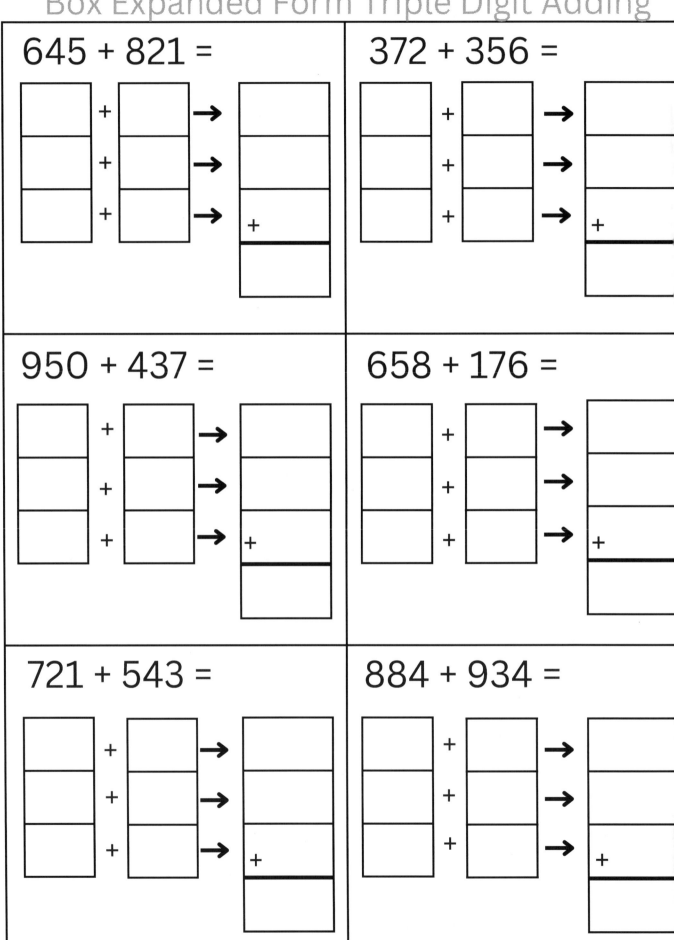

645 + 821 =

372 + 356 =

950 + 437 =

658 + 176 =

721 + 543 =

884 + 934 =

Box Expanded Form Triple Digit Adding

863 + 437 =

215 + 443 =

485 + 214 =

936 + 725 =

656 + 343 =

179 + 146 =

374 + 825 =

752 + 264 =

590 + 147 =

863 + 618 =

237 + 394 =

689 + 200 =

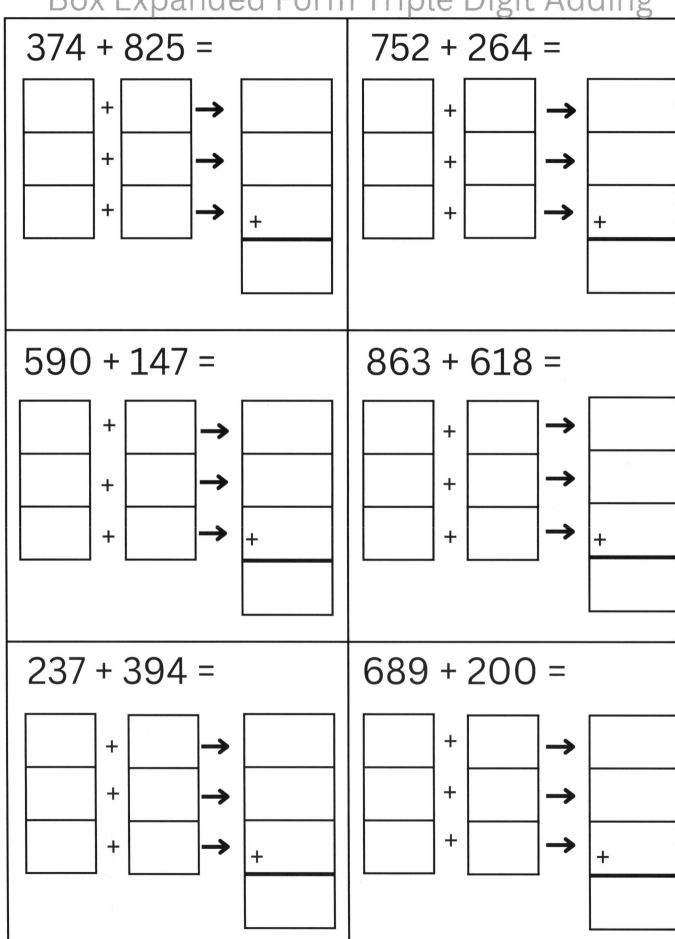

Box Expanded Form Triple Digit Adding

527 + 151 =

943 + 926 =

261 + 437 =

684 + 730 =

847 + 536 =

762 + 315 =

Box Expanded Form Triple Digit Adding

775 + 513 =

362 + 124 =

590 + 208 =

176 + 832 =

937 + 465 =

248 + 236 =

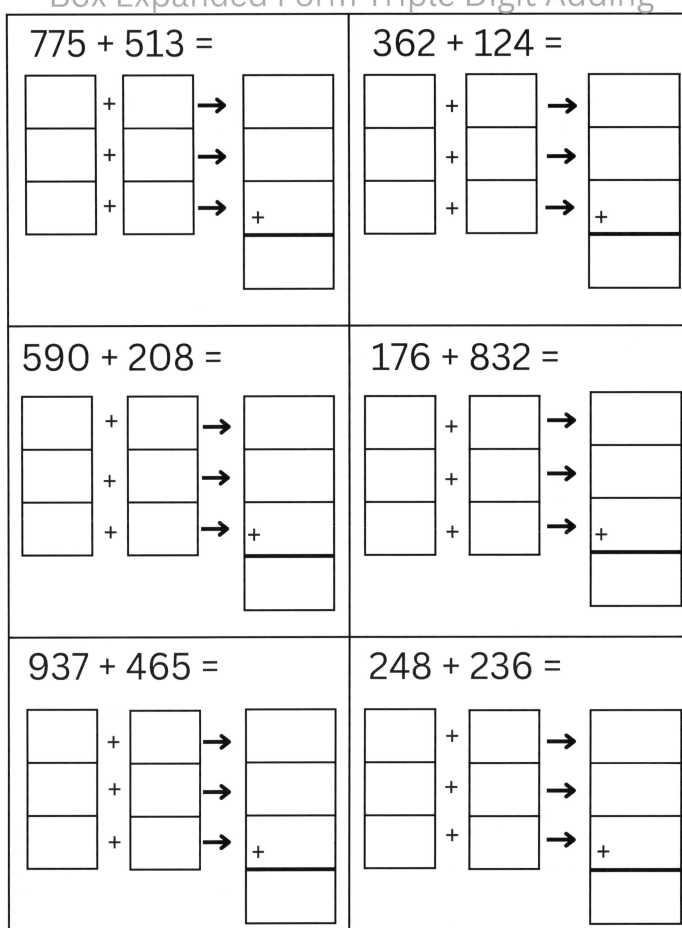

Box Expanded Form Triple Digit Adding

937 + 642 =

514 + 361 =

608 + 371 =

249 + 500 =

872 + 546 =

463 + 215 =

Box Expanded Form Triple Digit Adding

183 + 413 =

742 + 835 =

564 + 627 =

161 + 284 =

900 + 378 =

327 + 340 =

Box Expanded Form Triple Digit Adding

294 + 957 =

538 + 370 =

621 + 744 =

375 + 413 =

183 + 208 =

746 + 825 =

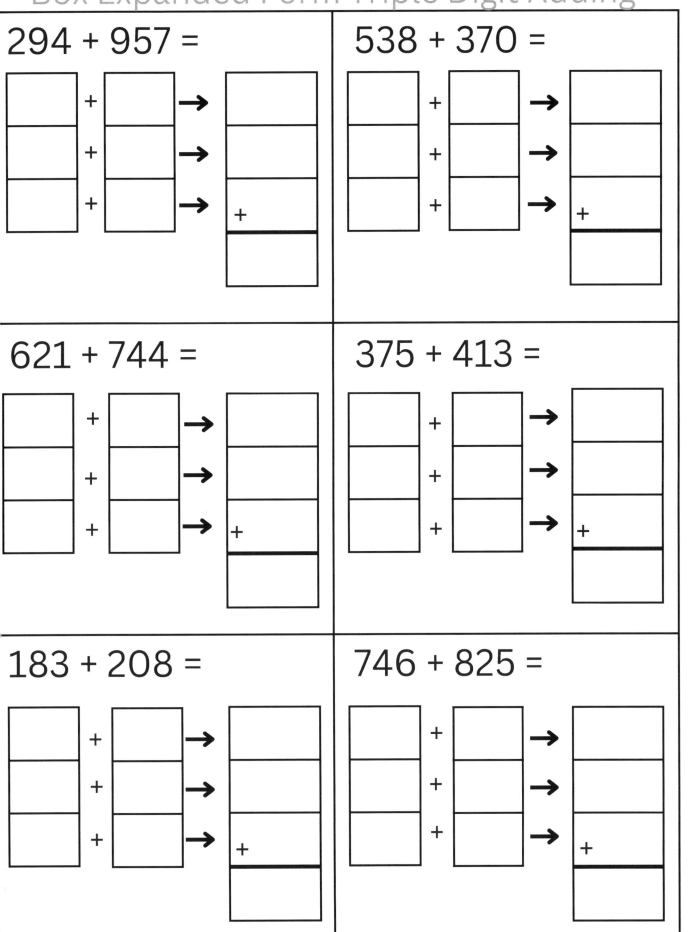

Box Expanded Form Triple Digit Adding

489 + 300 =

720 + 264 =

254 + 913 =

863 + 531 =

371 + 726 =

940 + 638 =

Box Expanded Form Triple Digit Adding

658 + 732 =

373 + 158 =

198 + 820 =

743 + 415 =

452 + 936 =

812 + 340 =

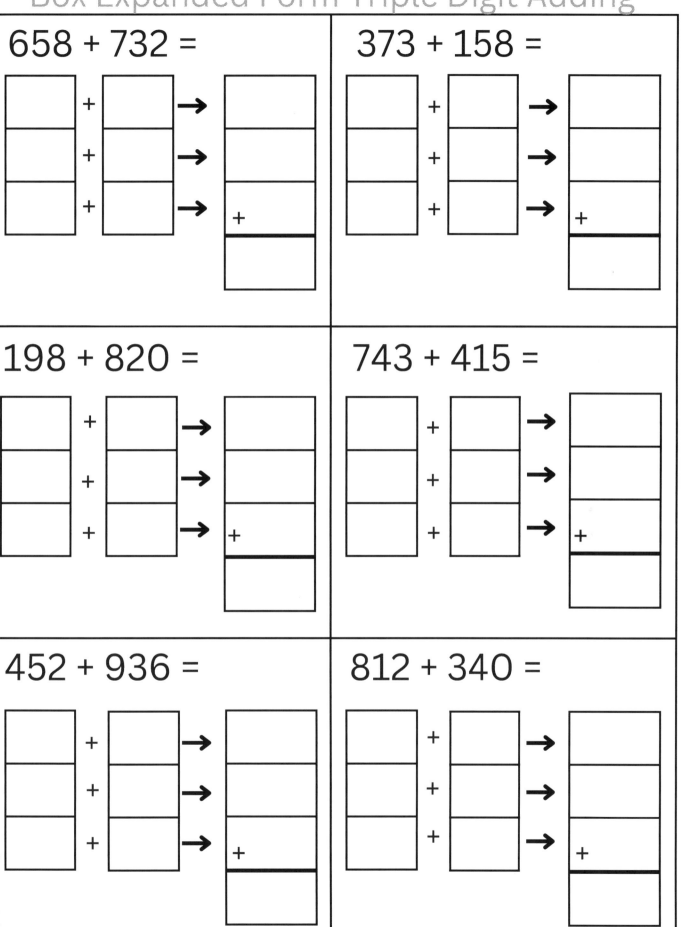

Box Expanded Form Triple Digit Adding

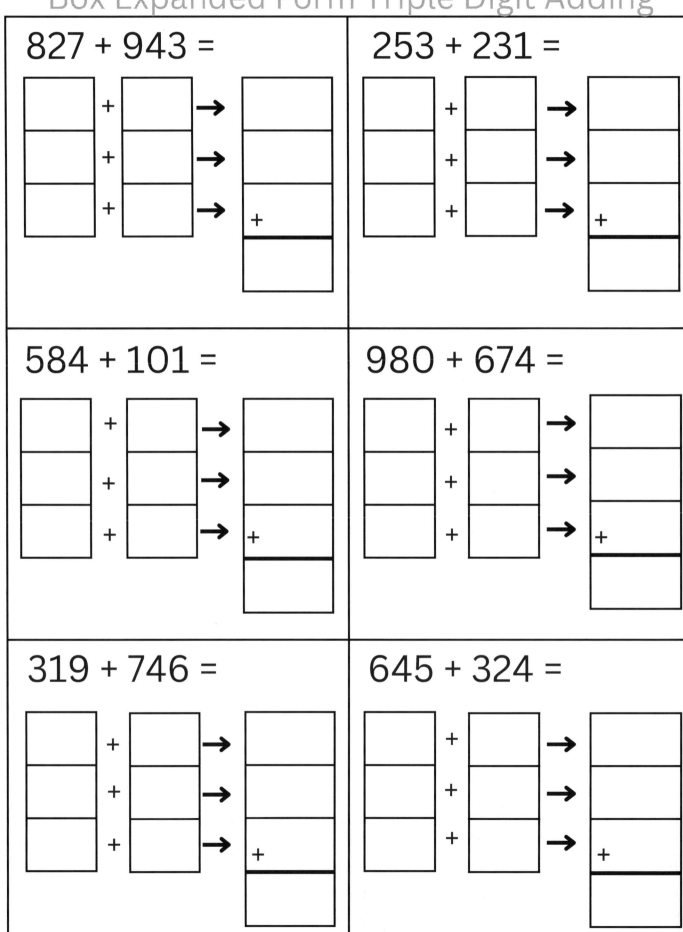

827 + 943 =

253 + 231 =

584 + 101 =

980 + 674 =

319 + 746 =

645 + 324 =

Box Expanded Form Triple Digit Adding

147 + 321 =

583 + 304 =

718 + 456 =

846 + 721 =

931 + 174 =

620 + 598 =

Box Expanded Form Triple Digit Adding

390 + 307 =

745 + 573 =

976 + 684 =

164 + 281 =

831 + 756 =

482 + 873 =

Box Expanded Form Triple Digit Adding

639 + 741 =

284 + 404 =

567 + 943 =

703 + 356 =

319 + 874 =

965 + 786 =

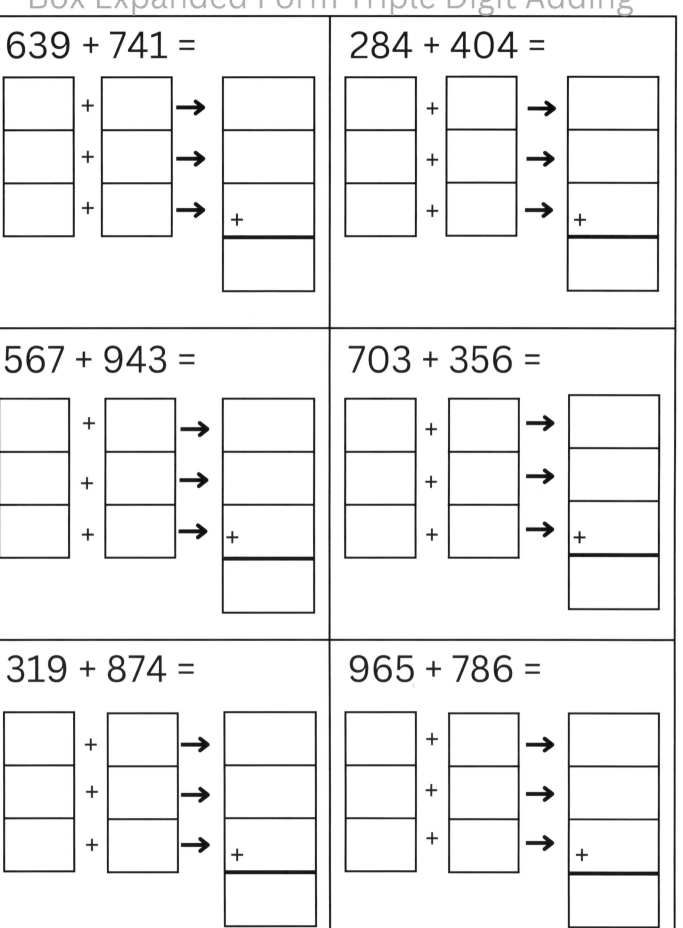

Box Expanded Form Triple Digit Adding

823 + 694 =

476 + 453 =

294 + 187 =

175 + 503 =

961 + 743 =

358 + 210 =

Box Expanded Form Triple Digit Adding

179 + 610 =

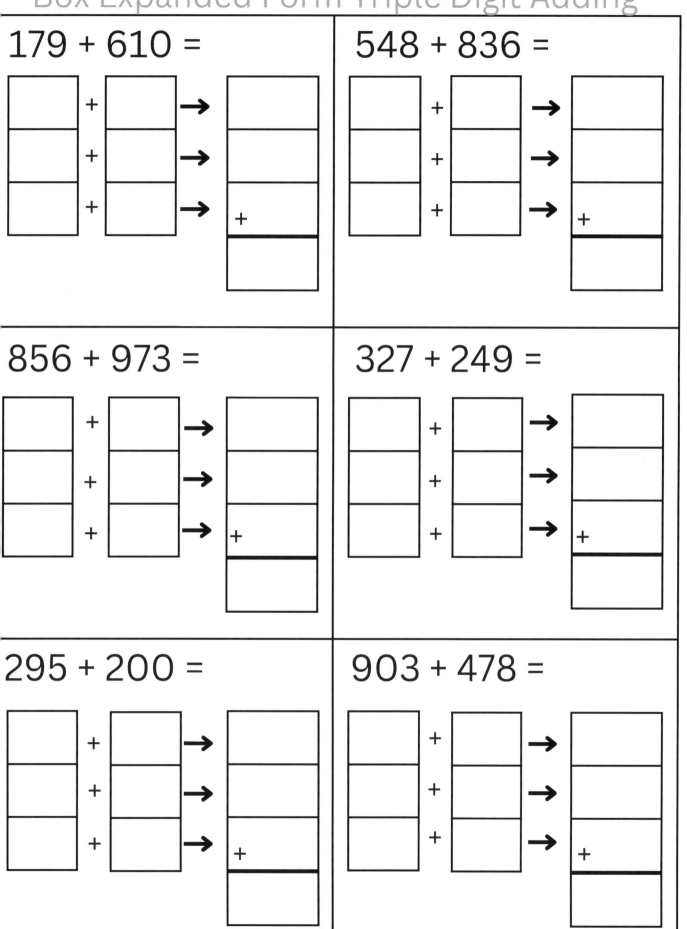

548 + 836 =

856 + 973 =

327 + 249 =

295 + 200 =

903 + 478 =

Box Expanded Form Triple Digit Adding

374 + 936 =

762 + 143 =

957 + 768 =

136 + 461 =

482 + 305 =

849 + 582 =

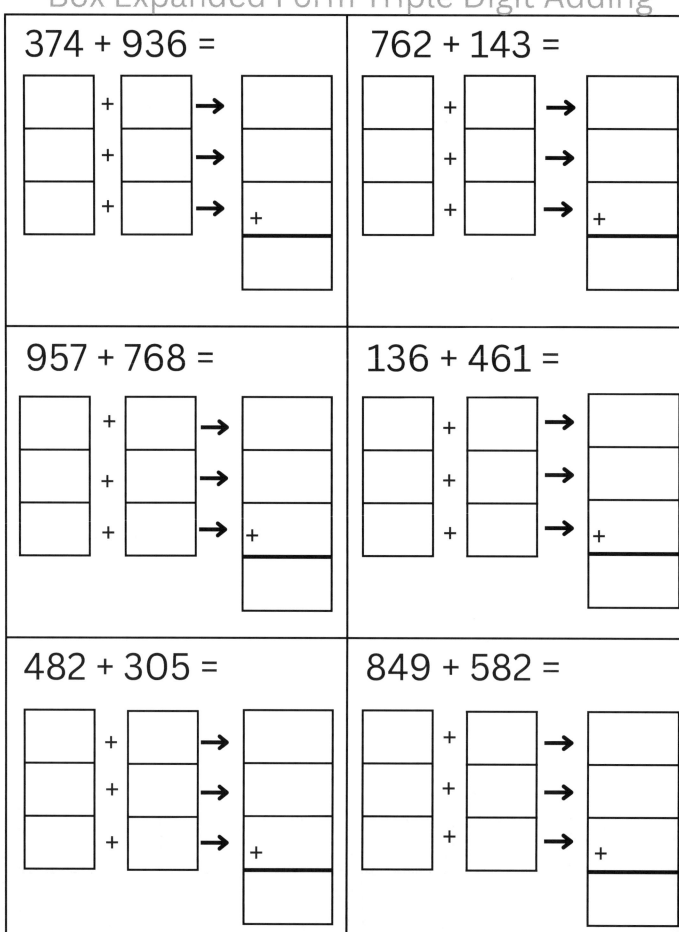

Box Expanded Form Triple Digit Adding

564 + 872 =

821 + 263 =

276 + 301 =

463 + 534 =

189 + 410 =

901 + 684 =

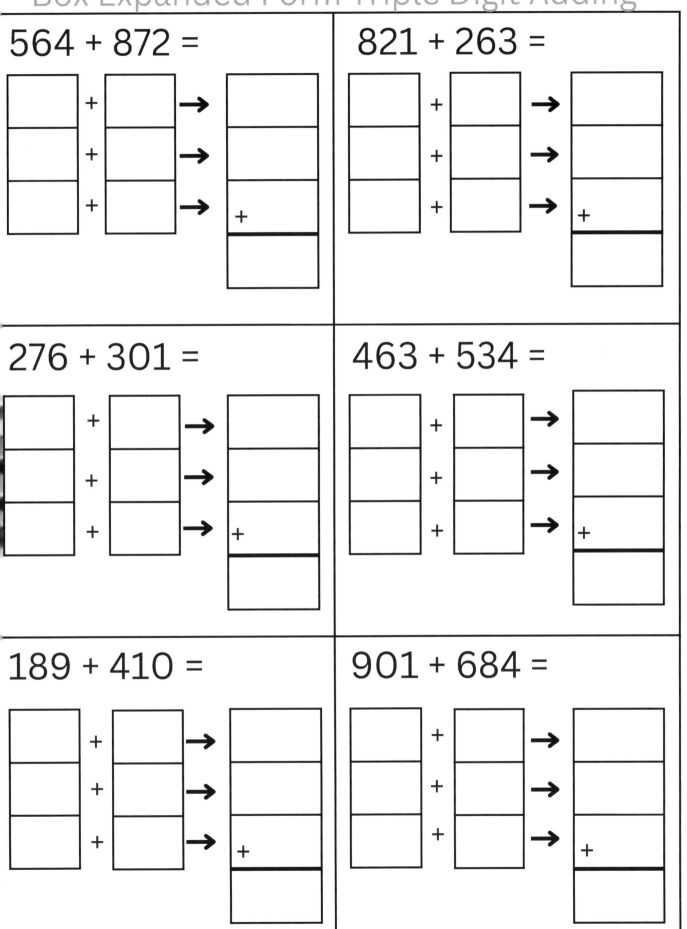

Box Expanded Form Triple Digit Adding

736 + 602 =

364 + 382 =

167 + 138 =

528 + 200 =

641 + 935 =

809 + 481 =

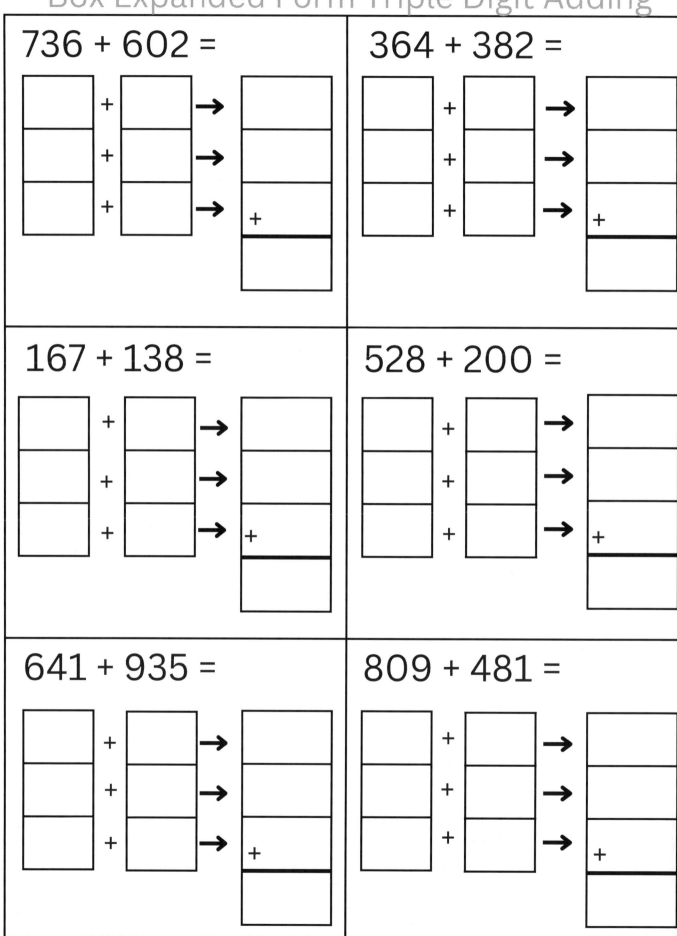

Box Expanded Form Triple Digit Adding

947 + 713 =

463 + 539 =

215 + 632 =

372 + 583 =

864 + 472 =

784 + 326 =

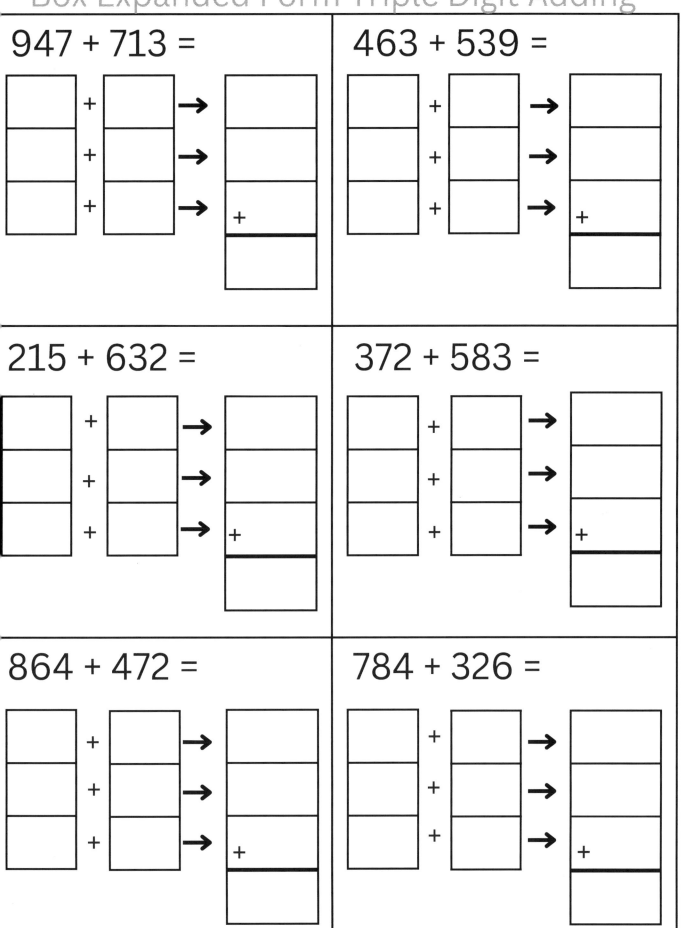

Box Expanded Form Triple Digit Adding

271 + 503 =

583 + 714 =

764 + 321 =

958 + 360 =

372 + 103 =

132 + 726 =

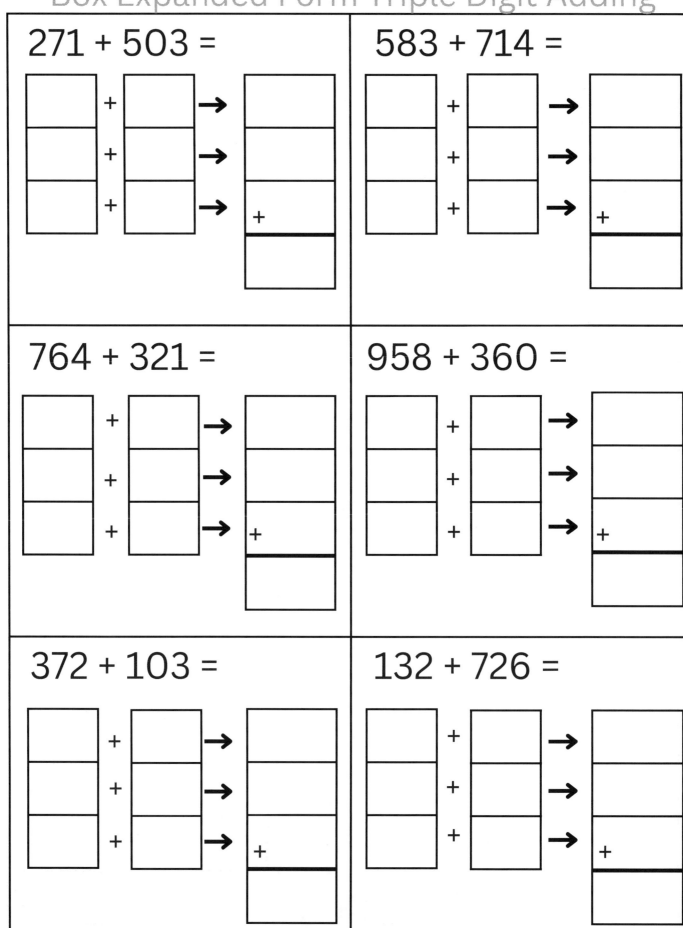

Box Expanded Form Triple Digit Adding

490 + 763 =

732 + 193 =

850 + 936 =

274 + 301 =

176 + 358 =

587 + 812 =

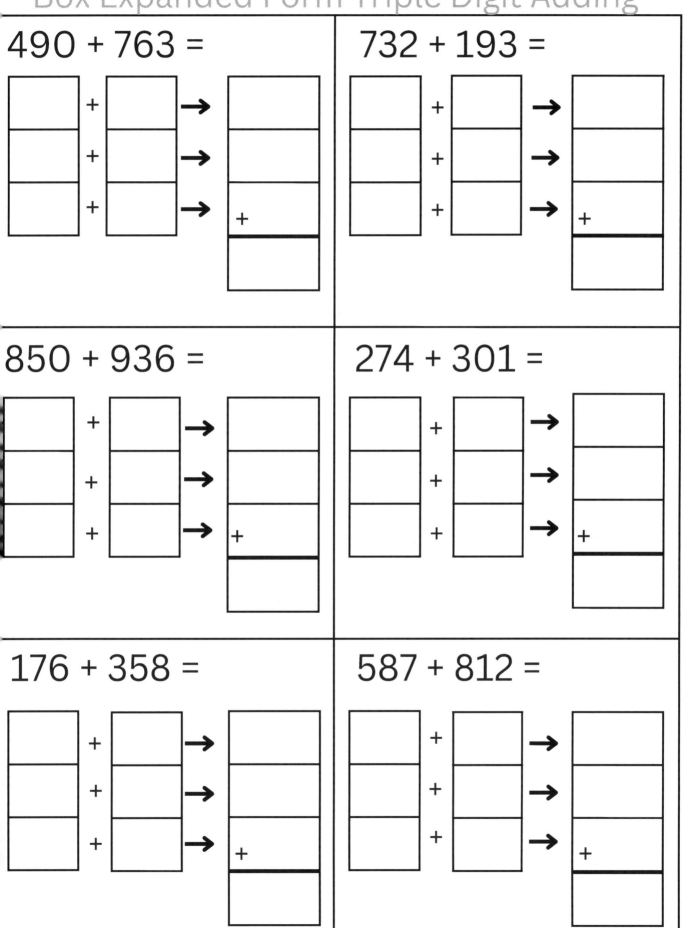

Box Expanded Form Triple Digit Adding

682 + 763 =

341 + 193 =

165 + 936 =

274 + 510 =

176 + 402 =

587 + 246 =

Box Expanded Form Triple Digit Adding

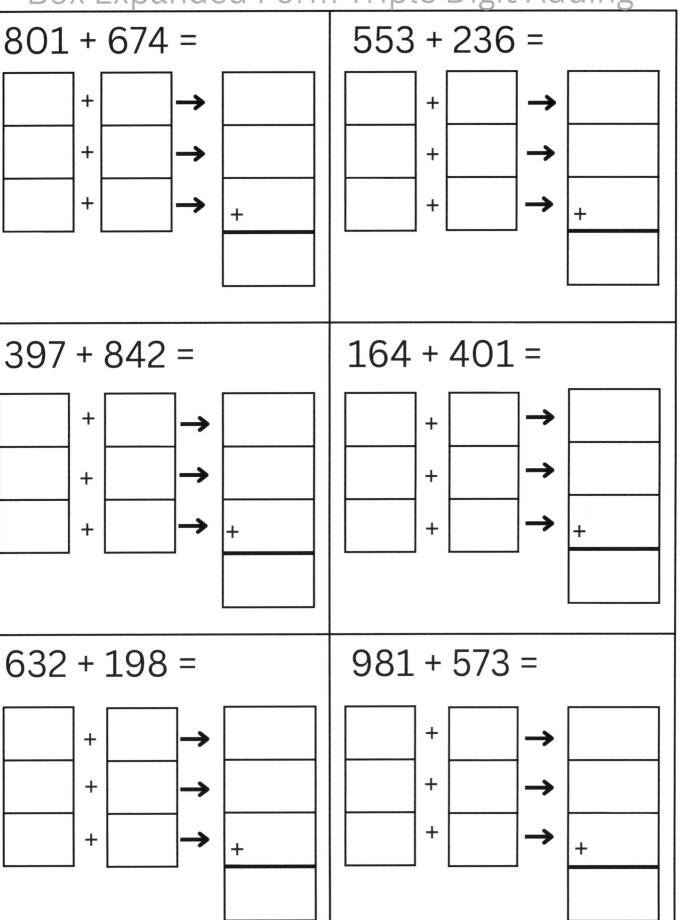

801 + 674 =

553 + 236 =

397 + 842 =

164 + 401 =

632 + 198 =

981 + 573 =

Box Expanded Form Triple Digit Adding

187 + 163 =

```
[  ]  +  [  ]  →  [      ]
[  ]  +  [  ]  →  [      ]
[  ]  +  [  ]  →  [      ]
                    +
                  [_____]
```

734 + 472 =

```
[  ]  +  [  ]  →  [      ]
[  ]  +  [  ]  →  [      ]
[  ]  +  [  ]  →  [      ]
                    +
                  [_____]
```

563 + 741 =

```
[  ]  +  [  ]  →  [      ]
[  ]  +  [  ]  →  [      ]
[  ]  +  [  ]  →  [      ]
                    +
                  [_____]
```

308 + 952 =

```
[  ]  +  [  ]  →  [      ]
[  ]  +  [  ]  →  [      ]
[  ]  +  [  ]  →  [      ]
                    +
                  [_____]
```

921 + 863 =

```
[  ]  +  [  ]  →  [      ]
[  ]  +  [  ]  →  [      ]
[  ]  +  [  ]  →  [      ]
                    +
                  [_____]
```

295 + 201 =

```
[  ]  +  [  ]  →  [      ]
[  ]  +  [  ]  →  [      ]
[  ]  +  [  ]  →  [      ]
                    +
                  [_____]
```

Box Expanded Form Triple Digit Adding

396 + 842 =

582 + 647 =

167 + 502 =

403 + 798 =

845 + 132 =

200 + 387 =

Box Expanded Form Triple Digit Adding

591 + 934 =

873 + 120 =

284 + 304 =

926 + 851 =

370 + 416 =

142 + 222 =

Box Expanded Form Triple Digit Adding

729 + 146 =

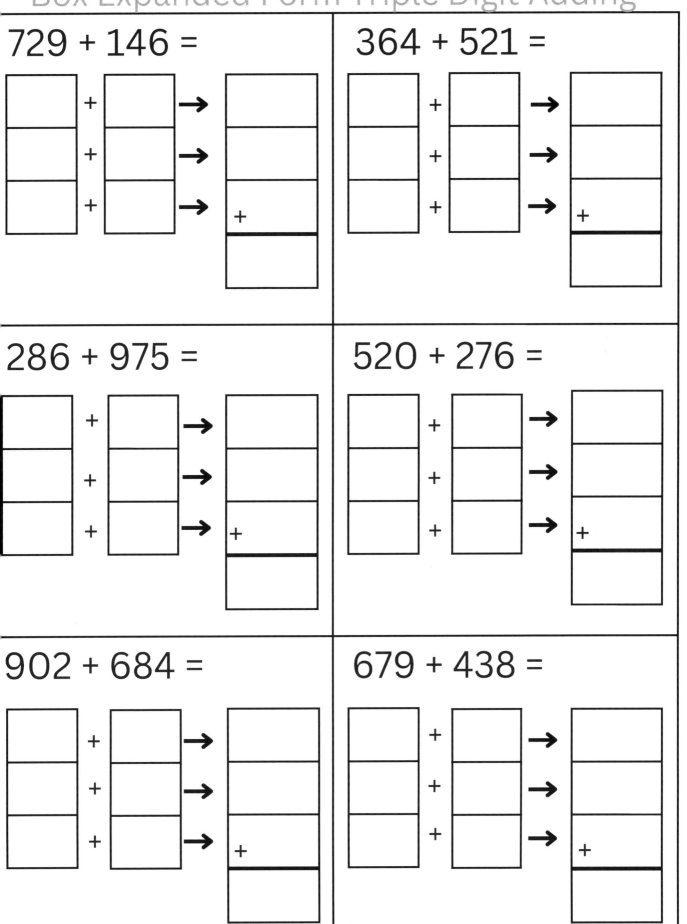

364 + 521 =

286 + 975 =

520 + 276 =

902 + 684 =

679 + 438 =

Box Expanded Form Triple Digit Adding

923 + 647 =

564 + 215 =

175 + 303 =

812 + 478 =

648 + 932 =

740 + 321 =

Box Expanded Form Triple Digit Adding

279 + 100 =

781 + 564 =

936 + 842 =

340 + 513 =

974 + 305 =

685 + 247 =

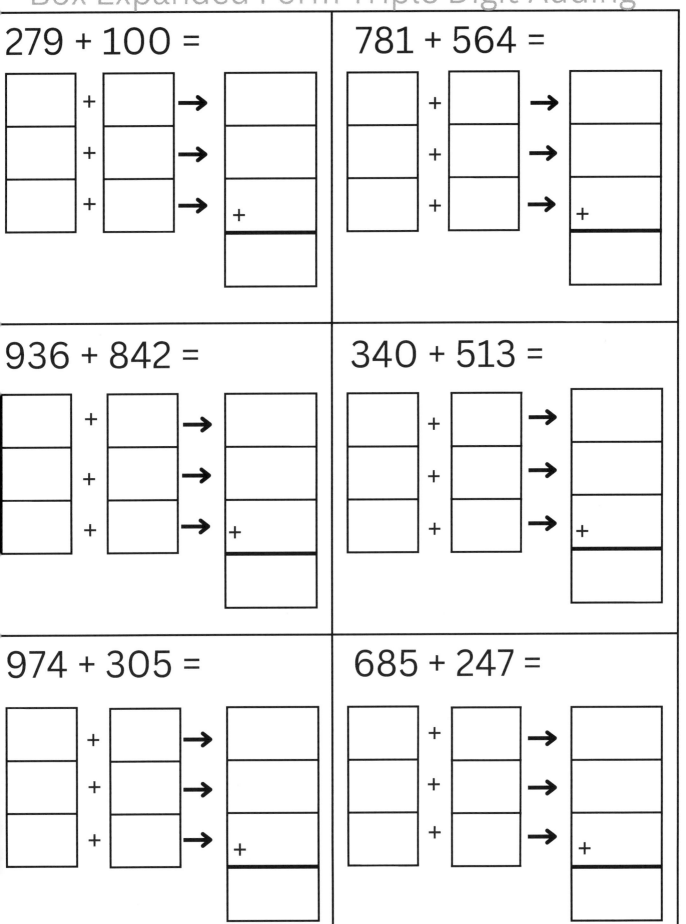

Box Expanded Form Triple Digit Adding

462 + 207 =

831 + 347 =

190 + 264 =

573 + 928 =

765 + 810 =

396 + 401 =

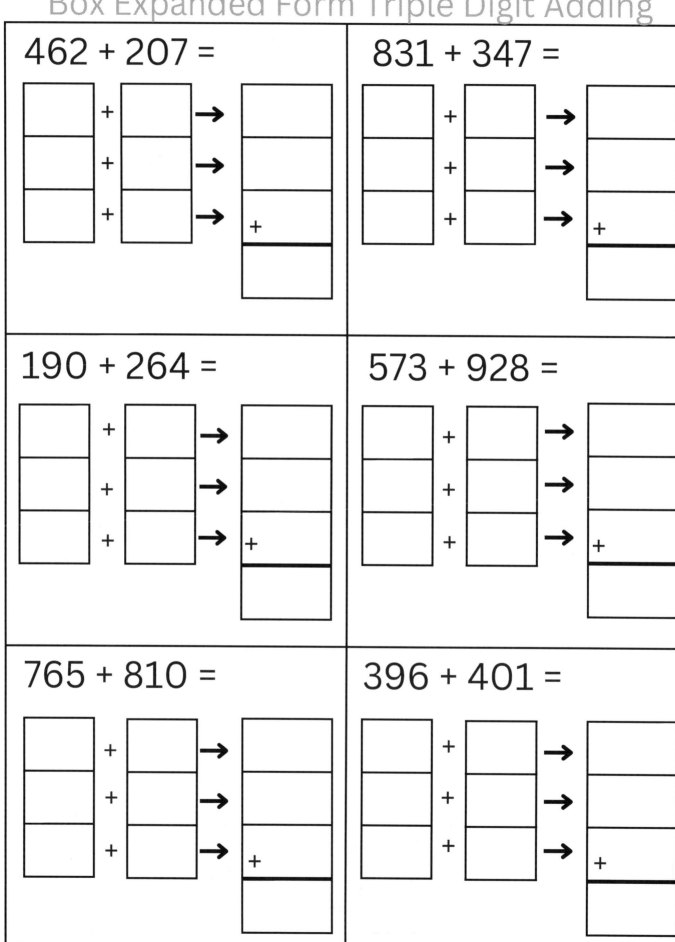

Box Expanded Form Triple Digit Adding

671 + 543 =

482 + 204 =

359 + 536 =

247 + 101 =

924 + 785 =

183 + 512 =

Box Expanded Form Triple Digit Adding

847 + 625 =

521 + 362 =

163 + 472 =

684 + 251 =

308 + 984 =

455 + 832 =

Box Expanded Form Triple Digit Adding

179 + 643 =

352 + 105 =

938 + 752 =

571 + 836 =

690 + 234 =

264 + 983 =

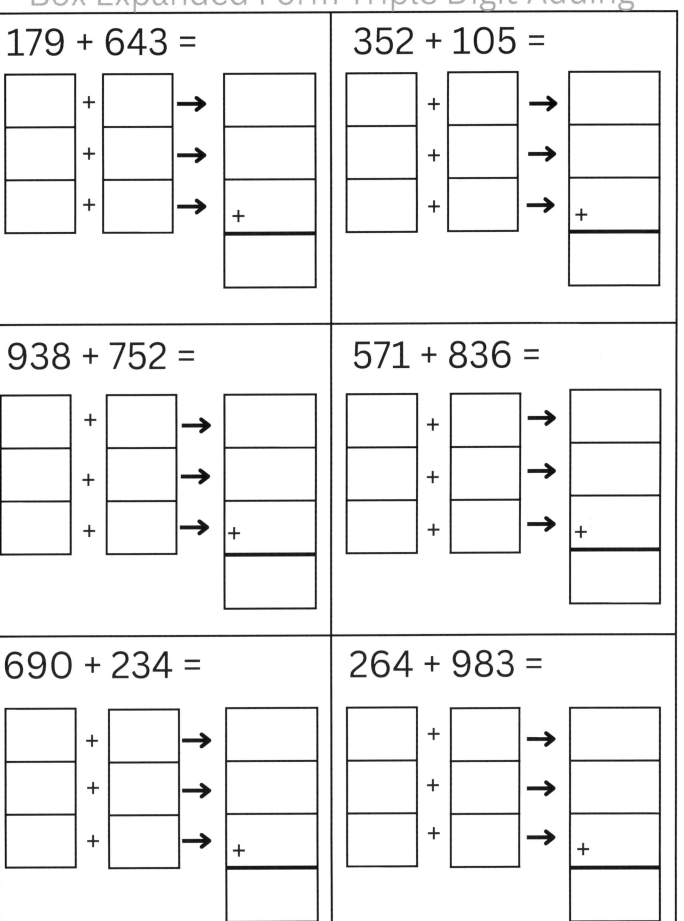

Box Expanded Form Triple Digit Adding

359 + 184 =

746 + 683 =

185 + 502 =

837 + 946 =

682 + 495 =

510 + 238 =

Answer Key

Answer Key

Day 1	
105	118
99	106
123	62
158	109

Day 2	
110	129
97	108
98	120
122	83

Day 3	
125	61
84	101
125	79
121	140

Day 4	
139	81
98	100
158	145
63	148

Day 5	
127	84
101	147
144	117
119	123

Day 6	
102	119
88	129
101	150
120	163

Day 7	
126	137
93	145
152	112
77	141

Day 8	
84	152
149	95
144	106
107	112

Day 9	
150	85
149	52
146	150
100	198

Day 10	
89	77
131	149
175	59
165	141

Day 11	
98	130
142	175
113	122
126	95

Day 12	
158	101
111	177
90	115
78	133

Answer Key

Day 13	
104	186
130	78
143	148
60	113

Day 14	
174	63
123	79
131	143
110	86

Day 15	
34	55
193	111
71	152
171	132

Day 16	
89	131
120	178
165	46
112	146

Day 17	
93	178
97	163
59	87
158	118

Day 18	
158	68
143	73
109	49
154	160

Day 19	
59	157
118	150
79	127
68	121

Day 20	
155	168
71	181
83	59
99	126

Day 21	
125	75
171	123
59	120
148	96

Day 22	
99	118
142	173
88	38
142	94

Day 23	
153	59
131	160
165	51
124	61

Day 24	
188	83
123	119
79	115
109	89

Answer Key

Day 25	
142	62
81	78
178	59
112	79

Day 26	
48	99
173	109
76	138
100	58

Day 27	
28	126
93	175
57	126
113	146

Day 28	
70	157
49	179
141	58
85	133

Day 29	
156	48
110	129
78	147
100	60

Day 30	
59	129
162	116
78	33
97	86

Day 31	
78	94
164	56
94	62
126	100

Day 32	
120	50
67	85
62	109
38	93

Day 33	
103	71
188	106
85	57
120	127

Day 34	
98	132
177	33
76	166
115	107

Day 35	
87	113
161	49
114	157
59	130

Day 36	
48	123
98	105
50	89
67	187

Day 37	
140	98
130	124
75	162
116	49

Answer Key

Day 38	
860	1,157
1,251	1,732
924	775

Day 39	
1,133	926
1,568	1,120
985	1,259

Day 40	
1,466	728
1,387	834
1,264	1,818

Day 41	
1,300	658
699	1,661
999	325

Day 42	
1,199	1,016
737	1,481
631	889

Day 43	
678	1,869
698	1,414
1,383	1,077

Day 44	
1,288	486
798	1,008
1,402	484

Day 45	
1,579	875
979	749
1,418	678

Day 46	
596	1,577
1,191	445
1,278	667

Day 47	
1,251	908
1,365	788
391	1,571

Day 48	
789	984
1,167	1,394
1,097	1,578

Day 49	
1,390	531
1,018	1,158
1,388	1,152

Day 50	
1,770	484
685	1,654
1,065	969

Day 51	
468	887
1,174	1,567
1,105	1,218

Day 52	
697	1,318
1,660	445
1,587	1,355

Day 53	
1,380	688
1,510	1,059
1,193	1,751

Answer Key

Day 54	
1,517	929
481	678
1,704	568

Day 55	
789	1,384
1,829	579
495	1,381

Day 56	
1,310	905
1,725	597
787	1,431

Day 57	
1,436	1,084
577	997
599	1,585

Day 58	
1,338	746
305	728
1,576	1,290

Day 59	
1,660	1,002
847	955
1,336	1,110

Day 60	
774	1,297
1,085	1,318
475	858

Day 61	
1,253	925
1,786	575
534	1,399

Day 62	
1,445	534
1,101	784
578	833

Day 63	
1,475	789
1,239	565
830	1,554

Day 64	
350	1,206
1,304	1,260
1,784	496

Day 65	
1,238	1,229
669	1,201
977	587

Day 66	
1,525	993
588	1,777
786	364

Day 67	
875	885
1,261	796
1,586	1,117

Day 68	
1,570	779
478	1,290
1,580	1,061

Day 69	
379	1,345
1,778	853
1,279	932

Answer Key

Day 70	
669	1,178
454	1,501
1,575	797

Day 71	
1,214	686
895	348
1,709	695

Day 72	
1,472	883
635	935
1,292	1,287

Day 73	
822	457
1,690	1,407
924	1,247

Day 74	
543	1,429
687	1,783
1,177	748

1st Grade Math Workbooks

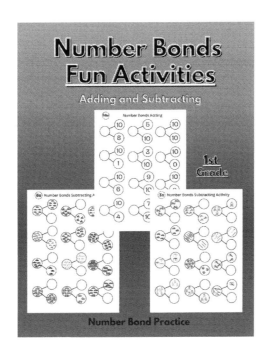

Made in the USA
Columbia, SC
28 February 2024

32351732R00048